UN-DUE WEST

D0067027

UN-DUE WEST

By Roland Sodowsky

Illustrated by Michael Krone

CORONA PUBLISHING CO.
SAN ANTONIO, TEXAS 1990

For information address:
Corona Publishing Co., 1037 S. Alamo, San Antonio, Texas 78210.

FIRST EDITION

Designer: Kathleen Giencke

Acknowledgments
"Rodeo," "Knobity," and "Brandpainting" were first published in the *Concho River Review*; many thanks to Terence A. Dalrymple, editor, and the Fort Concho Museum Press, San Angelo, Texas. "Boots" was first published in *The Atlantic*.

Thanks are due to Sul Ross State University, the Yaddo Colony, and the National Endowment for the Arts for their support and aid.

Library of Congress Catalog Card Number: 89-82343
ISBN Number: 0-931722-77-2

Manufactured in the United States of America.
10   9   8   7   6   5   4   3   2   1

Table of Contents

For some good friends and critics, the past and present members of Wordwrights in Alpine, Texas; for Joel and Barney Nelson of the Kokernot Ranch, who stand for the best of all things cowboy; and for all the real cowboys everywhere who are part of a tradition so rich that it can inspire even a maverick book like this and take it right in stride.

UN-DUE WEST

SIX-GUN I
Slowing Down the Trigger Finger

On a stifling August afternoon in 1873, Randall Sanchez and Cesar Hamaker burst out of the Sotol Saloon onto the dusty main street of Lindisfarne, Texas. Both Sanchez, a handsome redhead from the Shumacher Ranch, and Hamaker, the dark, dreamy-eyed assistant brandpainter of the Merton Ranch, were widely known as congenial, good-humored young cowboys, but now their features were contorted with anger. In voices thick with rage, Hamaker shouted hair-raising insults at Sanchez as they strode to the center of the street, which was quickly vacated by other pedestrians, and Sanchez replied with derisive, equally unforgivable taunts. Deliberately, menacingly, they backed slowly away from each other until they were about twelve paces apart. They turned, crouched, and dug their boot-heels into the dust as if rooting them forever. Their faces were gray with hatred and death. Their quivering hands hovered like fatal birds of prey over the box-holsters strapped to their thighs.

"You son of a bitch, draw!" Cesar Hamaker shouted, and thus began the longest and most famous gun duel in the history of the Texas Occident.

Handguns have been part and parcel of life, and occasionally death, in the Texas Occident ever since the arrival in the Chihuahuan Desert of those first hardy pioneers from the snowdrifts of New Hampshire. Fiercely proud of their constitutional right to bear arms in order to defend their homes and their way of life, every rancher and cowboy in the

Occident carried and still carries a side arm. The inevitable result has been that few denizens of the Occident have not encountered, outside a saloon or jazz bar or poetry-reading in Lindisfarne or some other desert town, that unbearable tension when, in the throes of anger over a real or imagined insult or injustice, two brave men faced each other a short distance apart, hands suspended above their holsters for what seemed like eternity before a devastating moment of truth burst upon the frightened street.

Most of the men in the Occident preferred the famous Colt .45, the handsome pistol with the revolving breech invented by Samuel Colt and patented in 1836. It is an efficient and dangerous weapon, capable of firing six deadly lead projectiles in rapid succession. Since almost every man on the range, in the bunkhouses, in the saloons, and in the streets had a Colt revolver strapped to his leg, the ranchers and cowboys soon realized that responsibility, good judgment, and self-discipline were needed among all the armed men. As early as 1858, three years before the Civil War, public forums were held monthly in Lindisfarne to discuss the six-gun's role in Occident society.

"We wanted to thrash out a policy by which we all could live, and of course I mean *live* in the literal sense," Miguel Cervantes, the foreman of the Kalplish Ranch, wrote to a friend many years later. "In our discussions, which often lasted until daybreak the next day, we quickly unearthed a paradox: every man there asserted over and over his unwavering faith in his fellow man's good judgment with regard to the miniature repeating cannon hanging from his belt, but no one had such faith in himself. Many times a cowboy shook his head doubtfully and said, 'I trust Hurley Perkins and Juan Dirksen, and everybody else. But I don't know about me and this killing tool here. I've got a nasty temper; what if my temper gets the better of me sometime, what if it turns into five seconds of murderousness? I don't want that to happen.' And as often as a man spoke of such fears, many others nodded in agreement."

The discussions led to the formulation of four elementary principles. These principles were later referred to as the Box-Holster Pact, although that pact evolved nearly eight years after the principles were first stated in a declaration printed in the Lindisfarne *Weekly Gatherer* on February 8, 1861. It was never really a pact at all but an unspoken general agreement, arrived at after several years of experimentation, as to the manner in which the ranchers and cowboys would carry their weapons.

The principles were as follows:

1. A lot of us have bad tempers.
2. They're so bad that sometimes we might even shoot somebody in the heat of the moment.
3. When we get mad we need a way to cool off before we do something dumb.
4. The way for us to cool off is to have something to slow us down between the mad-as-hell stage and the shooting-killing stage.

Various strategies to lengthen the time between the flashpoints of anger and of guns were tried over the next seven years. The War between the States, of course, which began in April of the same year the principles were published, temporarily suspended the experiments. Shortly after the end of the war, in the fall of 1866, Tad Kalplish I, owner of the Kalplish Ranch, proposed that, when two men became embroiled in an argument, their friends simply tie them up and refuse to release them until their anger subsided. Others pointed out, however, that the potential combatants might not always have friends with them, or if one man was with friends who tied him up but the other was alone, the action of a man's own friends might result in his death. So the Kalplish Solution was rejected.

In the same year Alfonso Vela, a cowhand on the Shumacher Ranch, suggested that they all carry blanks in their guns and ammunition belts, but this idea, known as the Vela Cap Pistol Notion, was also quickly rejected.

"We felt it was an unmanly way out of the dilemma," Cervantes wrote. "Eventually Alfonso, after much reflection, agreed. The point was that if, in an unpleasant situation, we had the option to use a gun, but the gun was harmless, then the option was meaningless, and we were deprived of our higher humanity. We had an elemental human problem, our tempers, which could, assuming we had real bullets in our guns, lead us to fatal results. Our higher humanity demanded that we use our integrity and intelligence not to lead us to such a fatal and intrinsically stupid end. If there were blanks in our guns the whole crisis deteriorated into silliness, and we would be left without dignity."

The first positive step forward came the next year, in 1867, with the introduction of Macleoud's Holster Gum, an extremely strong and tenacious, never-drying glue which was invented by Angus Macleoud, the famous pioneer bootmaker. Its application was simple: using a paddle furnished with each jar of glue, the gun owner tamped and packed the stiff, viscous substance into the holster around the gun. Presumably, after that he need never fear again that he would shoot too soon. Delighted ranchers and cowboys were soon thronging Macleoud's bootshop, and, within two months after its introduction, the *Weekly Gatherer* reported that more than eighty percent of the men in the Texas Occident had their guns glued in their holsters.

"Let us congratulate ourselves," the *Gatherer* exulted in a front-page editorial on October 20, 1867; "we are entered into a new era in which we no longer must fear our own natures."

The false bubble of their new security burst in a hail of gunfire on a beautiful Saturday morning in Lindisfarne in April, 1868. On that morning, Manuel Perkins was across the street from the Sotol Saloon in Hubschrauber's General Store buying tickets to *Tristan und Isolde*, the first Wagnerian opera to be performed in Lindisfarne. Manuel, a cowboy on the Merton Ranch and the older brother of Hurley Perkins, the Kalplish Ranch wrangler, became involved in a heated argument with Ramon Slape, one of the seven barefoot Slape brothers, over Slape's sister, the petite and beautiful Lupita Nell. It was a tragic, classical case of mistaken identity, for Hurley, not Manuel, had been secretly paying court to Lupita Nell. Manuel repeatedly denied Ramon Slape's accusations, but the exchange became uglier and increasingly abusive until it spilled out of Hubschrauber's Store onto the street, and the two men tugged at the pistols glued in their holsters.

At first glance, it would have appeared to be a one-sided duel, as indeed it was, although not on the side that anyone who knew the two men would have expected. Manuel Perkins was a small, dapper, rather cold-eyed cowboy, cool and sure in every movement and gesture, and a deadly marksman with his Colt .45. On the other hand Ramon Slape, a hairy, burly giant of a man, had never been known to hit anything even with the ten-gauge shotgun which he occasionally carried, much less his pistol.

But as witnesses who had crouched behind hogsheads and hitching posts along the street reported later, everyone had forgotten one important fact about Macleoud's Holster Gum: strength was required to pull the gun from the glue-filled holster, and Ramon Slape was several times stronger than Manuel Perkins. With little more than a contemptuous grunt, he extracted his gun from its holster and began shooting at Manuel, thirty or forty feet away, while the smaller man pulled desperately at his mired revolver. Slape missed six times; cursed, reloaded, missed six times again, and then a third time. In the meanwhile, as bullets whizzed by or kicked up dust around him, Manuel had removed his gun-belt, sat on the ground, braced his feet against the holster, and was pulling on the revolver with both hands, but he had not even gotten the hammer above the top of the holster. Still, however, Slape continued to miss, and if fate had not intervened in the form of Betsy Hubschrauber, Manuel might have killed him an hour or so later.

Betsy was a tall, broad-shouldered woman who wore many large bows on both her bonnet and dress. Widely regarded as contentious and not a little greedy, she was miffed because the argument had turned into a gunfight before she could complete the sale of the opera tickets. She was sure that she would sell only one now, because one buyer or the other would be dead. She had been watching the duel from the safety of her store, but after Ramon had missed and reloaded several times, she stepped out on the porch.

"Hell, Ramon," she shouted, "You couldn't hit an outhouse from the inside."

"Do what?" Ramon swung around to look at her, and as he did he accidentally pulled the trigger again. The bullet struck Manuel Perkins squarely in the chest. The duel was over, and ranchers and cowboys alike denounced Macleoud's Holster Gum, none more loudly than the remorseful, barefoot Ramon Slape.

Discouraged but no less determined to have their six-guns and their peace of mind too, the gun-bearers of the Texas Occident returned to their drawing boards. Two months after the Perkins-Slape tragedy, the Mayor Miranda Mitten, invented and marketed by the mayor of Lindisfarne, Panther Junction Miranda, offered a brief ray of hope. The mayor based his invention on the premise that a hand encased in a mitten sewn from a double layer of buffalo hide could draw, cock, aim, and pull the trigger of a pistol only with great difficulty. It would be so difficult, in fact, as to guarantee both the peace of mind of an Occident cowboy and the safety of his friends and enemies.

The mitten sold briskly for a few weeks until numerous complaints were uttered at the monthly meeting of the Texas Occident Society Against Plugging Each Other.

"My men can't work wearing these loathsome mittens," snapped Miguel Cervantes, the Kalplish Ranch foreman. "It's like having just one hand."

Rudolfo Miller of the Merton Ranch said, "They're hot, too. It ain't sensible to wear a mitten in August in the desert."

"You think you've got it tough," sneered Ralph Garza, also of the Merton Ranch; "what about us fellows that are ambidextrous? We have to wear the damned things on both hands."

Reluctantly and regretfully, the Mayor Miranda Mitten was rejected too, and gloom descended over the TOSAPEO meetings, "So thick," Miguel Cervantes wrote, "you could've bagged and sold it for mattress stuffing."

The breakthrough came four months later in the Shumacher Ranch bunkhouse, a few days before Christmas. Arturo Shumacher I, the flamboyant, narrow-booted rancher, had gone to the bunkhouse after supper to help the cowboys string popcorn for Christmas tree decorations. He relates the story:

"Valentine Finch, our foreman, had bought all the crew members boxes of dominoes for Christmas. He sat on the floor behind his bunk to wrap his presents while the rest of us were working around the Christmas tree, a handsome juniper. We were singing Christmas carols. When Valentine finished, he brought his presents over and put them under the tree. Of course we all knew right away from their distinctive rectangular shape what they were; he gave the same thing every Christmas. We pretended ignorance, however, even when one young cowboy, Carrasco van Deventer, picked one up and shook it.

" 'Put that down, Carrasco,' Valentine said.

"Instead, Carrasco stuck it in his holster. He had left his pistol in Lindisfarne to have the barrel blued, for the Macleoud Holster Gum had badly discolored it. So he stuck the box in his holster, and then he uttered the word that galvanized all our minds, that caused us to coalesce in one splendid moment of spontaneous inspiration.

" 'Draw!' Carrasco said to Valentine, his hand suspended over the gaily-packaged domino box. Valentine stared at him, and we stared at him, and he at us, all of us open-mouthed. And then with one voice we shouted, 'Eureka! That's it!' "

The "It," after many modifications in the next six months, became the Shumacher Mixed Gun- and Bullet-boxes and Box-scabbards, better known collectively as the Texas Occident boxes and box-holsters, or simply the toxboxes.

The equipment consisted of two cast-iron boxes, each about the size and shape of a domino box, carried by the cowboys in similarly shaped holsters. One box held the cylinder of a Colt .45 and cartridge cases and bullets, the other the rest of the revolver and powder for the shells, so that one opened box was useless without the other. The toxboxes were padlocked, and the keys — the locks required different keys—were given to a friend.

"Thus we achieved a built-in cooling-off period," Miguel Cervantes wrote to his friend. "By the time a would-be duelist found his friend with the keys, unlocked the boxes, assembled the revolver, and made his own cartridges, we felt, most men would regard their quarrels in a different light. Some cowboys felt that we should give the keys to enemies, rather than friends, for safe-keeping, but others thought this to be an overly gratuitous gesture, given the safeguards we had already devised. Besides, few of us had enemies anyway. One small faction, noting a tenuous similarity of conception to that disreputable device of ancient times, wanted to call the toxboxes Killer Chastity Belts, but they were quickly voted down."

By late spring of 1869, most of the technical problems involved in the manufacture of the toxboxes—the gauge of the metal, dimensions of the box, heft of the padlock, and so forth—had been worked out. By September of that year box holsters were being worn by every rancher and cowboy in the Occident. The first test of the devices came soon after, in October, when, after an exchange of derogatory remarks about the color schemes in their chaps, Rudolfo Miller of the Merton Ranch squared off with, ironically enough, Carrasco van Deventer of the Shumacher Ranch.

"They were at the Harnsgartner Tanning Salon when the disagreement began," Cervantes wrote. "Acquaintances quickly ran to find the friends who had the men's toxbox keys. Within half a day each possessed both his keys, and shortly thereafter had his revolver out and assembled. But after they had poured powder into their shells and were crimping the casings, they began to glance furtively at each other and to look more and more sheepish. Finally they both stopped making ammunition."

Rudolfo said, "Aw hell, Carrasco, I reckon mauve and green ain't such a bad combination for chaps."

Carrasco replied, "I was just thinking, those coyote-fur strips dyed burnt-orange look real nice, now that I've got used to the idea. What say we put this damned shooting-iron stuff back in the boxes and go have a drink?"

Everyone in the Occident rejoiced. The *Weekly Gatherer* reported, "We have passed the acid test with flying colors; we have ascended to a higher plateau." And indeed, such was the case. Two months after the Miller-van Deventer confrontation ended in friendship without bloodshed, Angus Macleoud himself, the inventor of the ill-fated Holster Gum, stepped into the street to face Juan Dirksen of the Kalplish Ranch in a dispute about the height of the heels on a pair of boots Dirksen had ordered. By the time their keys-carrying friends could be rounded up a few hours later, the would-be duelists were engrossed in a chess game on the sidewalk and had forgotten their quarrel entirely. Similar duels began with such regularity and ended with such equally bloodless results over the next four years that the new era once heralded by the *Gatherer*, it seemed, had truly arrived, and, as Cervantes put it, "Serenity descended over the desert."

Serenity which remained undisturbed until that scorching August afternoon in 1873 when Randall Sanchez and Cesar Hamaker stepped into the street outside the Sotol Saloon and proceeded to prove that human stubbornness could unsquare the corners of the most carefully planned paradise.

"Stubbornness my granny; they're just a damn pair of pervicacious pigheads," Tad Kalplish II was to say fifty years later.

The Sanchez-Hamaker gun battle began in a dispute over a card game. Seated at a scarred and stained table in the Sotol Saloon, Sanchez and Hamaker were paired against Alfonso Vela, who, like Sanchez, worked on the Shumacher Ranch, and Leticia Harnsgartner, the sister of the Lindisfarne postmaster. Leticia had come to Lindisfarne from Hartford, Connecticut, to visit her older brother in the spring of 1866. She soon learned to love the vast, wild desert spaces and the rugged starkness of the mountains, and she stayed to establish the first house of prostitution in Lindisfarne. Later, she also opened the Harnsgartner Tanning Salon.

"One club," Sanchez said.

"One heart." Leticia removed Sanchez's hand from her knee.

"Three no-trump," Hamaker said.

Sanchez slammed his cards down on the table. "That is the dumbest bid a man ever bid since God made creosote bush."

"I reckon if anybody'd know dumb, it'd be you," Hamaker replied, half-rising from the table and edging his hand toward his box holster. "And you'd know about molesting ladies' knees that ain't wanting to be molested, too."

Leticia and Alfonso managed to placate the hot-tempered young men, and the game continued. Both Sanchez and Hamaker were believed to be secretly in love with the sultry, long-lashed Leticia—as indeed were many other love-starved cowboys in the Occident—and each jealously watched the other's furtive attempts to steal caresses from her, smiles, or even a brief glance from the deep blue pools beneath her canopied lashes. Twice more, Sanchez and Hamaker half-rose from the table after one or the other had made an over-obvious advance toward Leticia, and twice more she and Alfonso calmed them down.

Then Alfonso made a fatal error. Trying to re-direct the conversation, he said to Hamaker, "I sure like that avant-garde brandpainting you did on Persephone III. Are you going to do that on all the Merton Ranch cows?"

"Avant-garde my dirty socks," Sanchez sneered. "Persephone III's probably died of shame from having that Pre-Raphaelite archaism splattered on her flank. She's the laughingstock of the Occident."

For half a minute Randall Sanchez and Cesar Hamaker stared at each other in a silence that bellowed with peril. It seemed like eternity to Alfonso and Leticia.

"You're a dead man," Cesar said.

"We'll see," Randall replied, and they headed for the door of the saloon.

(Continued: see SIX-GUN II)

BOOTS

The first United States settlers in the Texas Occident were from New Hampshire. They were fruit and nut gatherers of English and Scottish descent who had for many centuries worn high, open-topped boots in which to drop their food as they gathered it. This tradition was continued in the Occident, where a gatherer's specialty could usually be ascertained by the color of his boot-tops, since, over a period of years, the seeping juices of the fruit and nuts stained the leather. Green mesquite beans, for example, produced a bright chartreuse color still popular among cowboys today; dry mesquite beans produced a rich mahogany stain, darker than that of pecans; the rosy pink-red stain, also still popular, was produced by prickly pears and blood.

Many puzzled historians have noted that the Texas Occident boot resembles the contours of the human foot about as much as bandannas do bananas. Searching for a reason why anyone would commit such violence on his own feet, some historians have mistakenly assumed that the Texas Occident boot was worn by devoutly religious cowboys as a form of penitence, like flagellation. Its severe discomfort, however, may be traced to a singular chain of events involving two men, Angus Macleoud and Arturo Shumacher II.

Macleoud was the first bootmaker in the Occident. He settled in the once-thriving community of Lindisfarne, set to work building a bootshop, and, like many of his comrades from New Hampshire, sent for his family, as well as for his bootmaking tools. He had traveled lightly on his trip westward in search of a new home. Unfortunately, the immigrant wagon train bringing Macleoud's family was attacked by Comanches on the Middle Concho River southwest of San Angelo, and his wife, his ten-year-old daughter Marie, and all his boot lasts except a pair for women's boots were taken. His wife was never heard of again. One of the lasts reappeared later in Galveston as a result of the infamous Comanche sweep to the Gulf in 1878; it had been sharpened and attached to a lance which wounded Augustus Kalplish, a Galveston land speculator. Macleoud had etched his name on the last, so it was traced to him in Lindisfarne, and Kalplish sued him for damages under the Attenuated Responsibility Act in the well-known "Last Laughs" case, but was awarded only one dollar, and the last was returned to Macleoud, who immediately put it to use again.

Since many pioneers had lived in the Lindisfarne area for several decades without new footwear, demand for Macleoud's boots was intense. Using his last for women's boots, which had been filed to a point, Macleoud produced boots for men and women alike as fast as he could make them, despite their sharp toes and uncomfortable, unstable, and impractical high heels. By the time other bootmakers had arrived in the Texas Occident, the tradition was established, and they were forced to throw away the lasts designed for more reasonable and healthy low-heeled footwear in favor of the regional fashion.

"It was a love-hate relationship," Miguel Cervantes recalled many years later. Cervantes was the philosopher-foreman of the Kalplish Ranch and one of a handful of men who had been in the Texas Occident long before even the pioneers such as Macleoud had arrived; had, in fact, "been here forever, I reckon."

Cervantes continued, "We all hated Macleoud's boots. The heel would wobble out from under you without warning, and at the worst times; your toes always hurt. The boot always fit too tight, and your feet would sweat and then smell like—well, like they'd been in a cowboy boot all day. The tops were too gaudy for most of our tastes. Even that little trifoliate stitching on the toe that was Angus' trademark was a mistake; he

was homesick for maple trees, so he tried to do a maple leaf, but it looked more like a sprung fleur-de-lis. But you get used to a thing, you know; we all cussed and swore we were going to buy tennis shoes, but we never did."

Unreasonable though they were, the first generation of boots that Macleoud made were nevertheless more comfortable than those of the next, thanks to the flamboyant young heir to the vast and ancient Shumacher Ranch, Arturo Shumacher II. By 1884 Arturo II was already one of the most popular figures in the Occident. Notwithstanding his strangely shaped feet, which, a contemporary wrote, "were as slender and sharp as yucca blades," he had won everyone's admiration with his gracious manners, his quick wit, and his uncanny ability to find hackberries. It was this talent which, indirectly, resulted in his becoming one of the indelible legends of the Occident.

On August 23, 1884, Arturo II was picking hackberries near Horseshoe Springs when he espied Angus Macleoud's daughter Marie in a Comanche encampment. Emptying the hackberries from his boots into a hollow cottonwood tree, he concealed himself in the thick willows along the creek and awaited his chance to rescue her. That opportunity came when, as most of the camp slept in the heat of the afternoon, Marie approached the creek near where Arturo II was hidden. She glanced around carefully and then removed her large and elaborate earmuffs, which she had been wearing since leaving New Hampshire many years before.

Arturo II was stunned.

"She was wildly beautiful," he wrote many years later in Volume II of his autobiography. "For many minutes I could only gaze as she washed her thick, lustrous black hair. Then I remembered that the short time I had in which to save her was rapidly running out. I burst from my concealment, dashed across the shallow creek, threw her over my shoulder, and began that long, desperate race across the desert toward Lindisfarne."

Actually, as Marie was to note in Volume III of *her* autobiography, which was written after Arturo II's death, the creek was not as shallow as her rescuer had reckoned, and he had to empty his boots of several gallons of water before he could even move, much less throw Marie over his shoulder. By the time he had poured the water out, she had recovered somewhat from her surprise at having a young, flamboyant stranger speaking a language she barely remembered burst from the willows wearing such outlandish footwear.

"He threw me over his shoulder and began running," Marie wrote, "but I recalled that I had left behind some ornaments for my earmuffs that I especially treasured. So I made him go by my tepee for them. Then he set out again, but I had another thought and made him go back to the tepee once more for a large, soggy, rather messy parcel that I also coveted."

By then, of course, the whole encampment had been alerted, and as Arturo II set out at a dead run in a southwest direction across the desert with Marie thrown over his shoulder, all the Comanches in the camp came howling after them. After two or three miles they began to catch up, partly, Marie wrote, "because Arturo II was carrying me, but more because of his strange footwear, which made running nearly impossible."

Taking a bite from the soggy parcel they had returned for, Marie chewed for a moment and then said to Arturo II, "I'm very curious about something, and since the Comanches are about to catch us, and kill you, perhaps you should tell me now. Where are you taking me?"

"Why, to your father, Angus Macleod, in Lindisfarne," Arturo II panted.

"Oh." Marie jumped lightly down from her uncomfortable position over his shoulder. "Why didn't you tell me before? I can run much faster than you, and we can easily outdistance our pursuers, if you'll take off those ridiculous boots."

Arturo II glanced at his boots and pondered for a moment as arrows began to whiz all around them. Then he shook his head. "I couldn't do that. Tradition, you know."

"So," Marie concluded, "I grabbed him, threw him over *my* shoulder, and commenced running across those trackless wastes again. The Comanches soon lost heart then, for they knew I had the bear's strength and the hummingbird's speed, and they could never catch me."

Thus Marie was reunited with her father. Now sixteen years old, and, in addition to being wildly beautiful, also addicted to raw buffalo liver, which was what the parcel they had returned for contained, Marie was married in October to Arturo II in the most elaborate wedding ever seen in the Occident. Macleoud, who was immeasurably grateful to Arturo, went into seclusion in his workshop a month before the wedding and crafted the young man a pair of boots especially designed for his dainty, spear-shaped feet.

At the wedding, hundreds of impressionable young men, all, if the truth be known, secretly and hopelessly in love with Marie, watched Arturo II and Marie swirling gracefully in the center of the ballroom floor at the Shumacher Ranch. Long before the wedding week was over and Arturo II and his bride had departed to retrieve his cache of hackberries, Macleoud had more orders for the thin, impossibly pointed boots than he could ever hope to fill in his lifetime. Many young men performed radical operations on their feet by their own hand, cutting off all or parts of several toes to achieve the desired foot configuration, and the practice has continued in some remote areas of the Texas Occident to this day, although most parents prefer to shape their infant sons' feet by binding them.

It has never been determined why some people began to call the Macleoud boot a "cowboy" boot in the early 1920's; conservative Texas Occidentals still refer to it by its traditional name, the fruit boot.

BARBED WIRE

A Texas Occident rancher vacationing in England caused an uproar in the British press a few years ago. "It's nice countryside," he said, "but these stone walls and hedges are poor substitutes for barbed wire fences." The outraged cries of "Barbarian!" illustrate the widespread misapprehension of the meaning of barbed wire to Texas Occidentals. In no other way are they more misunderstood and unfairly judged.

The London reporter who overheard the rancher apparently ignored his next statement, for it never appeared in print: "Stone walls and hedges are occasionally beautiful in their dark, alternately geometric and irregular patterning over the green hills; but they merely say, 'this side is mine, that is yours.' What you see is what there is, no more; whereas our airy staves of barbed wire sing of beauty, of form within form."

That cattleman was Tad Kalplish III, and he knew whereof he spoke, for both his father and grandfather had been among the handful of men in the Texas Occident who, in the second half of the nineteenth century, determined that a fence should be more than a fence.

Ironically, the first fences in the Occident were indistinguishable from those Kalplish had criticized in England. Both rock and thorny desert brush extremely suitable for hedging were in greater supply than anything else, and ranchers quickly made use of these natural materials. One may still find, extending for many hidden miles in the dark arroyos and canyons of the Big Bend area, meticulously crafted stone fences, their walls faultlessly plumbed, their tops sloped for drainage, many of

17

them six feet high and nearly as wide. And what were clearly mesquite, juniper, or cactus hedges also persist, now overgrown, of course, but man's disciplining touch is evident in their right angles, their unwavering path across drywash and gulley, over rimrock and rockslide.

The first recorded complaint against these fences appears in a journal entry made by Tad Kalplish I, who wrote, "May 10, 1854—Was talk in saloon of fences & hidges [sic], some men asking their purpose, whilst others cursed their sameness." It is almost certainly no accident that this discussion took place in 1854, for news of the patenting in November 1853 of Meriwether Snake Wire, produced in New Braunfels, Texas, must have spread quickly and reached Lindisfarne and other towns in the Texas Occident by the following spring, implanting the seed of a concept so sweeping as to be in a state of perpetual manifestation even today.

The next mention of fencing is in the minutes of the Lindisfarne township meeting for October 20, 1859:

> Mr. Kalplish of Cabora Creek: These fences in uglie monotonie of morter'd rocke do sufocate manie blades of grasse, yea the verye land itselve, & set neigghbor gainst neigghbor.
>
> Mayyor Hon. Miranda: Keepe they not the cattle close-penned?
>
> Kalplish: Nay, we pen not oure cattle, for they should be free as we.
>
> Mayyor Hon. Miranda: Showe they not ownershippe and portecte from trespasse?
>
> Kalplish: Nay, we are not fickel about such smalle things. Everye man is wellcome to traverse oure land.

Those words were spoken on the eve of the War between the States, and fences were forgotten until several years afterwards. The story picks up again in Kalplish's journal: "April 8, 1869—Still unable to find Meriwether Snake Wire, but heard from Arturo Shumacher of a wire called Kelley's 2-point Diamond Point and have sent Miguel to San

Antonio, or beyond if necessary, to find and bring same."

In March 1871, after noting the birth of his son, Tad II, Kalplish wrote, "Miguel has returned dismayed, as are we all; Kelley's 2-point Diamond Point wire is armored with sharp barbs which would tear the skin of man or beast. Miguel refused to buy a single foot of it, and rightly so."

But barbless wire proved difficult to find, as the entries in Kalplish's journal over the next two decades attest:

> June 20, 1877—We are in receipt of Watkins 4-pt Lazy Plate Wire, of Merrill's Holdfast Twirl, & of Missouri Hump; all, alas, are barbed.
>
> October 1878—In receipt of Scutt's Clip, Billings' 4-Point, Underwood Tack Wire. All barbed except Underwood, which is savagely armor'd with tacks.
>
> February 1880—Our foreman Miguel has taken a liking to Crandal's Champion Galvanized with continuous triangular points. "See how sharp they are," I remonstrated; "why do you like the vicious things?" He replied, " 'Tis their triadic quality; something of eternity there." But I said no to this wire also.
>
> November 11, 1884—Ellwood 2-point Spread, Waukegon 2-point Half Round, Baker Fish Mouth, & Nadelhoffer's Twist, all barbed. The world forces barbed wire upon us. Miguel and our wrangler Hurley Perkins much interested in the Nadelhoffer's symmetry, parallel strands with barbs extending outwards each side.
>
> July 1887—Hodge Spur Rowel, armed with small sharp rowels. We are falsely accused of gouging our horses with our boot spurs; would we spur our beloved cows with our wire?
>
> July 1888—Pooler-Jones Single Line 3-Point, barbed.
>
> April 1892—Allis Flat Ribbon, barbed; what shall we do?

What they did was done in a furious onslaught of inspiration and energy during the Great Blizzard of 1893. Tad Kalplish II, nearing twenty-two by then, had just returned from Lindisfarne when the storm struck. A long entry in Kalplish I's journal relates the events of the following week which were to profoundly affect the Texas Occident:

> January 23, 1893—I scarcely know where to begin. Twelfth January Tad II returned late of the night, the north wind already bitter cold & great snowflakes falling. He said we had no choice but to fence, for State & Federal Gov'ts were building roads & without fences as guides would locate them willy-nilly, for their surveyors are a soft-headed, foolish lot.
>
> Snow fell all the next day & all the next; day was more night than day, & more snow was here than ever before beheld. Nor man nor beast could move from where he was. Tad II & I began to crave the sun, for we neither had lived two days before without seeing it, & we feared for Miguel and the others in the bunkhouse, how their provision fared. The third day it snowed still, as we could see from our second-floor windows, & we despaired for the men.
>
> But at midday came a knocking at the kitchen door & 'twas Miguel, who had tunneled unerringly through the snow from the bunkhouse. We quickly brought him food, but he shook his head, saying, "I have something to show you," & showed us several yards of Waukegon 2-point Half Round wire with the point of every barb bent over & tucked & blunted so smoothly it would not harm a baby.
>
> "The men have done this joyfully for two days and wax ever more skillful," he said. Tad II & I held the wire & felt it many times, & all our melancholy fell away. We made shift to bring the men food, but Miguel said, "They will not eat." He borrowed my magnifying glass and returned to the bunkhouse.
>
> After midnight he roused us from sleep, saying, "Look what Hurley Perkins and I have crafted." & we looked, & saw that they had rendered differently each barb of a three-yard strand of wire, one like an Ionian column & another Corinthian, one like a Gothic arch & another Norman, one like the David statue. But

those most pleasing were unlike any earthly shape, yet their shapes called to our minds the cheering sun, peals of music from cathedral organs, the sharp smell of tomato leaves & taste of vintage Bordeaux, the slipperiness of attic dust.

Miguel pointed to some barbs so shaped & arranged as to be either vertical or horizontal, square or rectangle, in perpetual harmony, like a wonderfully rational geometry. They were painted in the colors of the rainbow, yellow, red, or blue. "Those are mine," he said. Then he pointed to other barbs that in their shapes and colors dissolved to nothing, then re-formed as the very souls of light, hour, & season. "Those are Hurley's."

Tad II & I fell back, wordless. At last I said, "Is it possible?" & Miguel replied, "It is possible." We embraced, & Miguel returned to the bunkhouse, & I to bed.

But Tad II paced the house all the rest of that night, & morning came & it still snowed. He crawled through the tunnel to the bunkhouse & did not return that day or night. The next morning he returned & said, "Come with me," & I went, & saw that the men, working feverishly by candlelight, wild-eyed & ganted from hunger, had broken through the wall to the smithy, which was built against the bunkhouse, & young Roscoe Judson pumped the forge whilst Hurley & Miguel bent over the anvil with small hammers, needle-nosed pliers, fine chisels, & my magnifying glass. Mando Dirksen was crushing lumps of clay & rock in a metate and mixing them with oil for paint, & his older brother Juan was painting some barbs. They had torn out the floor of the bunkhouse from end to end & found posts somewhere & set them in the earth & strung five strands of wire. I saw the parallel wires were greatly like a staff of musical notation.

"Lovely," I said to Tad II, but he replied, "Look closer; look at each strand & then comprehend the whole."

I did so for many minutes, & the more I looked the more perforce I had to look, for the shape & color of every barb spoke of

themselves, & spoke together in horizontal succession along the wire, & spoke in vertical succession from strand to strand, & all together. The bunkhouse filled with light, whether from without or from the bright singing pentad before me I could not tell.

At last Hurley said, "The sun has come out," & I staggered back, overcome.

When I had recovered somewhat, I asked, "Can it be done? Can we fence all the canyons & mountains & flats thus, every barb of every strand profound & unique in form & song?"

"We can," Miguel & Tad II replied with one voice.

I shuddered at the immensity of the project. "My God, who knows how much time it will need?"

& Hurley said, "The cathedral at Chartres took two centuries."

I looked at each face in the bunkhouse then, Tad II, Miguel, & all the cowboys, & their eyes wavered not. "So be it," I said.

Long before the great snowdrifts had melted, the undertaking began, and continues today, the second and third generations of apprentices of Miguel and Hurley Perkins working ceaselessly in the low, adobe-walled barbshops along Cabora Creek and elsewhere.

Had the London reporter remained to hear out Ted Kalplish III, he doubtless would have been increasingly confounded, for Kalplish said, "No classes from English grammar schools spend whole days in subdued awe studying a fence on some dusty roadside, and weep when they must leave; people do not park bumper to bumper for miles on Sunday afternoons alongside some remote English hedge or stone wall. No English peasant covets a chance to walk beside hedges and stone walls for the rest of his life, but our cowboys beg to be line-riders and refuse to quit once they have these jobs, for as Arvil Judson, one of my line-riders, once said, 'It's like reading an ever-burgeoning epic, viewing a vast Van Gogh, and listening to a Copland symphony at the same time.' "

Kalplish concluded, "Many ask why we build a barbed wire fence straight up a boulder-strewn mountainside where not a blade of grass, not a mesquite or starving juniper grows, where no self-respecting goat, let alone a cow, would venture. We build them not to set a boundary, show title, or fend off the trespasser, but to satisfy that stern taskmaster Art, who insists on the truth of a raw cliff as well as the green meadow, who insists that neither the Taj Mahal nor a fence be left unfinished. Whether we are understood by the world at large matters little, for when was true and great Art ever understood, and when did true and great Art ever care?"

CHAPS

Legend has long since immortalized the hardships and heroism of the sturdy fruit and nut gatherers who in 1869 donned their warmest earmuffs and left the rolling green hills of New Hampshire forever, embarking on an erratic nine-year course of migration during which they crossed the Mississippi River five times, pushed as far southeast as Macon, Georgia, where four wagons were lost in the swollen Ocmulgee River, and as far back north as Lake Itasca in northwest Minnesota, where they crossed the Mississippi for the fifth and last time and turned southwest toward the inhospitable deserts and mountains of the Texas Occident.

"So caught up were we with the clamorous urgency to carve a life and home out of these rocks, cacti, ocotillo, and mesquites that the first years of settlement flew by," Angus Macleoud, the first bootmaker in the Texas Occident and a founder of the once-thriving town of Lindisfarne, was to write many years later. "When I look back now, days are scarcely distinguishable from years of taut struggle for life's elementary requirements: food to allay our hunger; adobe walls to fend off the biting wind, the merciless heat, the marauding Apache and Comanche; street, pillar, and steeple to proclaim our civilization."

So engrossed were the settlers of Lindisfarne and other towns in the Occident that it was not until the early 1880's that they began to question the utility of their earmuffs, which they had not removed since they left New Hampshire. Several argued that the intense heat of the region made earmuffs useless, even ridiculous, particularly in the summer months, and a motion was actually made and recorded in the April 1882 Lindisfarne town meeting that all citizens discard the superfluous garment. Two formidable forces, however, fashion and tradition, arose to unite the opposition.

Macleoud wrote, "One and then another, both men and women, had taken to ornamenting their earmuffs: a stray pearl from a necklace, a fresh bloom from a cactus pear, a concha and a bit of whang. Each month they were embellished more elaborately. And many who protested were shouted down with cries of 'See how lovely they are!' on the one hand, and 'Meddle not with our ways, the ways of our forefathers!' on the other. Even though the earmuffs of our forefathers had been plain as pancakes."

The motion was soundly defeated, and for two years Lindisfarners, even those who objected to the fashion, wore their earmuffs as usual. No one knew that, in a savage nomadic encampment to the north, a brave, lonely girl was behaving in an oddly parallel manner; nor did anyone suspect that she would soon have a dramatic and lasting impact on Lindisfarne fashions.

Angus Macleoud's ten-year-old daughter Marie had been taken in a Comanche attack on the immigrant train as it crossed the Middle Concho River in March 1878. She was rescued by Arturo Shumacher II, son of the prominent rancher, in a daring raid near Horseshoe Springs on August 23, 1884. By then sixteen years old and wildly beautiful, she had for six years successfully nurtured a superstitious fear and awe among her captors, who called her "Hairy-ears-that-grow," and later "Ears-like-hairy-tepee." Realizing immediately after her capture that her furry earmuffs had been mistaken for her ears, Marie had from month to month surreptitiously sewn on additional bits of buffalo and coyote fur. She decorated the ever-growing muffs with mesquite thorns, rodents' skulls, polished claws, tortoise shells, and bright stones to call attention to them.

Fortunately for Marie, the Comanches experienced extraordinarily good hunting in the year following her capture, which they attributed to Ears-like-hairy-tepee. They began to regard Marie as their hunting

spirit, benevolent and infallible, and soon her niche in the tribe was second to none. By the time Arturo burst out of the thick willows at Horseshoe Springs, threw Marie over his shoulder, and began the desperate race over the desert toward Lindisfarne, Marie's ears, or earmuffs, extended fully nineteen inches above her head and enveloped her like a cocoon, reaching to the ground.

"Marie's effect on Lindisfarne was galvanic," her understandably proud father wrote. "The first day she ventured forth from the bootshop after her ordeal, she walked alone in the street, alien as if she were come from the moon. Because of the expansion of her earmuffs, she could see only directly ahead, and that narrowly. She bumped into many people, and horses and carriages too, and all looked at her askance and backed away as her bones, tortoise shells etc. made a considerable rattling. But by the next morning every girl of Marie's age in Lindisfarne was similarly enshrouded, and bumping into this one and that, and by week's end everyone of every age wore earmuffs that hindered one's vision like a pair of leather walls, and everyone of every age was grievously bruised from interminable collisions."

Because of the isolation of Lindisfarne and other towns in the Occident, the fashion converted no one outside the area. Indeed, almost no one from elsewhere in Texas was aware of Occident earmuffs. While campaigning for governor in 1886, however, Lawrence Sullivan Ross came to Lindisfarne and was astounded to see the otherwise sane citizenry colliding with one another at every street corner because of their enormous earmuffs which, Ross muttered to one of his aides, "look like the damnedest horse blinders I ever saw."

Ross witnessed three injury-causing accidents in the short time he was in Lindisfarne. The experience apparently stayed with him, for he often inquired about conditions in Lindisfarne after he became governor in 1887. In 1889, after learning of a catastrophic earmuff-caused accident involving fifteen adults, six children, four wagons, eight horses, and three buggies, the exasperated governor issued an executive decree severely curtailing the popular Lindisfarne fashion.

"WHEREAS," the decree noted, "numerous injuries to the citizens, and widespread destruction of property belonging to the citizens of the Texas Occident, have occurred because of the wearing of earmuffs; and WHEREAS, while the Chief Executive is wholly cognizant of the beneficial aspects of the wearing of earmuffs, and of the sacred tradition underpinning the wearing of earmuffs, and of the hallowed inclination of the citizenry of the Occident toward the wearing of earmuffs, the Chief Executive has nonetheless become convinced of certain dangerous tendencies which the wearing of earmuffs do seem and are seen and have seemed to foster; THEREFORE the Chief Executive, after due consideration, does hereby on this day decree that the citizenry of the Occident, if the citizenry of the Occident chooses to wear them at all, be constrained and required to wear earmuffs which do not endanger life, limb, or property of themselves or others; and pursuant to this worthy purpose, the Chief Executive does decree that henceforth earmuffs may not be worn which extend above the waist."

Governor Ross was named president of Texas A&M University in 1890.

Arturo Shumacher II, who had married Marie Macleoud shortly after rescuing her, was in Austin at the time the decree was issued. Before he learned of it, however, he was surrounded by Texas Rangers as he left the Populist Hotel in downtown Austin. The Rangers advised him of the decree, and ordered him, then and there, to cut his earmuffs to the required dimensions or suffer immediate imprisonment.

As he sat on the sidewalk hacking at his earmuffs with a bowie knife, Shumacher was asked by a reporter who had followed the Rangers what he thought of the governor's decree.

"I'll tell you what I think," Shumacher snarled as he flung aside the useless and illegal top half of one earmuff; "I think it chaps me no end."

Thus was born the misnomer by which the world knows the leather garment that today decorates only legs, and which has been erroneously linked to the Mexican-Spanish word *chaparreras*. In the Texas Occident, however, tradition runs deep, and no cowboy has ever been heard to call his chaps anything but earmuffs.

SIX-GUN II
The Beginning of the Sanchez-Hamaker Gunfight

Ironically, in the summer of 1869 when everyone in the Texas Occident was changing over to toxboxes, the boxes which held disassembled revolvers and were to prevent cowboys from shooting each other before they had a chance to cool off, Randall Sanchez and Cesar Hamaker had each given the other the keys to his toxboxes. So when they squared off between the Sotol Saloon and Hubschrauber's General Store on that hot August afternoon in 1873, Randall couldn't shoot Cesar until Cesar gave him his keys, and vice versa.

"Give me my durn keys!" Randall shouted when they had faced off in the street.

"And you give me mine!" Cesar retorted.

Each began digging in his pockets, and then the ever-absent-minded Cesar remembered that he had given Randall's keys to Leticia Harns-gartner while he was swimming in a horse tank one idyllic afternoon the previous summer.

"Leticia!" Cesar shouted.

"What're you calling her for?" Randall snarled. Leticia had not followed the men outside to witness the shooting, and he suspected that Alfonso Vela was taking advantage of their absence by going upstairs with Leticia to her famous eight-sided bedroom over the Sotol Saloon.

"She's got your toxbox keys, that's what for," Cesar answered. "Now give me mine, so I can shoot you."

"I'm looking for them —" Randall began. Then he recalled that his pants had been stolen nine months earlier after a cattle drive to Ogallala, Nebraska, and that Cesar's keys had been in one of the pockets. "Oh, hell," he groaned.

"Oh hell what?"

"Kalplish!" Randall shouted. "Augustus Kalplish! Somebody go get Augustus for me."

"What are you calling him for?" Cesar asked. Augustus Kalplish, a cousin of the rancher Tad Kalplish I, was a former land speculator from Galveston who had established a highly successful detective agency in Lindisfarne.

Randall explained what had happened to his pants, and to Cesar's keys.

"Well, don't feel too bad," Cesar said. "At least you'll get your keys before I get mine and you can kill me. Leticia!"

Leticia was indeed busy with Alfonso Vela in her octagonal bedroom. Later in the afternoon, when she finally responded to Cesar's exasperated yells, she gave a little shriek and confessed to some absent-mindedness of her own. During brandpainting season, when her businesses were quite slow in Lindisfarne, she had gone home to Connecticut to visit her aging mother and her younger brother Amos, a prosperous banker. One morning, while she went for a dress-fitting in downtown Hartford, she had left the keys with Amos. She had returned to Lindisfarne without retrieving them.

With a quick apology to Cesar, Leticia ran to the Western Union office and dispatched a telegram to Hartford. She waited anxiously at the telegraph office, but no answer came that evening, or the next day.

In the meantime Valentine Finch, the foreman of the Shumacher Ranch, who was in Lindisfarne for his weekly appointment at the tanning salon, had found Augustus Kalplish and, acting for Randall, had hired the detective to find Cesar's keys. On the morning after the duel began, Kalplish left on the train for Ogallala to attempt to pick up the cold trail of the missing box keys.

Four days later, a telegram came from Leticia's mother, who was ill, advising Leticia that her brother had gone on vacation in the Catskills and could not be reached immediately.

While the searches for the two sets of keys proceeded, of course, the two men had not moved a muscle. They remained obstinately crouched in the street, their hands poised over their toxboxes.

A week after the fracas began, Randall asked Cesar, "You still mad?"

"I sure as hell am," Cesar answered. "I guess you might've been right about my bidding, and it don't make a whole hell of a lot of difference about Leticia Harnsgartner, but I ain't about to forgive you for what you said about my brandpainting on Persephone III, and if that detective you claim Valentine hired ever finds my keys, I'm going to blow your damned brains out."

Randall replied, "Well, I appreciate your seeing my point of view about the bridge game, and I agree with you about Leticia, but as far as I'm concerned, anybody that would imitate Rosetti's *Annunciation* on a cow's flank—and it was an abominably sorry imitation too—has insulted the cow, the ranch, and art in general, and deserves to die. If Leticia ever gets hold of her brother that you claim she claims went on vacation in the Catskills, and he sends my keys back, I'm going to shoot you so full of holes you'll look like a prairie dog town."

That was in mid-August. On the second day of September, Valentine Finch received a telegram from Augustus Kalplish, now in Kansas City. He was hot on the trail of a notorious pants thief named Cal Clinnjin. On September 8, Leticia Harnsgartner tearfully reported to Cesar that her brother apparently had not gone to the Catskills at all but on August 18, in Philadelphia, had boarded a train for Florida. He had been carrying his bank's cash—all of it—in a steamer trunk, and, presumably, also Randall's toxbox keys. However, Leticia assured Cesar, her mother had dragged herself from her sickbed and was now enroute to Florida to recover the keys.

In the meantime, during rainstorms on September 1, 4, and 6, a gutter extending from the roof of Hubschrauber's General Store had thrice filled Randall's left boot with water, causing it to shrink painfully on his foot. Cesar was faring better, although, on still days, the smoke from cigarettes which passersby obligingly lit and put in his mouth got in his eyes. He dared not, of course, lift either hand from its alertly hovering position over the box-holster to remove the cigarette.

On September 25 Augustus Kalplish telegraphed Valentine Finch that he was in Little Rock, Arkansas, still on the trail of Cal Clinnjin, and that he had narrowly missed cornering the pants thief in Joplin, Missouri. On the same day, from Miami, Florida, Leticia Harnsgartner's mother telegraphed that her son Amos had rented an entire floor of a plush resort hotel and entertained lavishly there for a week. He had checked out an hour before she, traveling almost literally with one foot in the grave, and the Florida state police had arrived. Mrs. Harnsgartner herself had been thrown in jail for two days on suspicion of being an accomplice, and after her release she was placed in a hospital for another two days, more dead than alive from the dank and dreadful conditions in the Miami jail. She had, however, recovered somewhat, and was once again pursuing her son, who was thought to have boarded a ship bound for the Bahamas.

Randall and Cesar's determined stand in the street while their keys were being rounded up had begun to attract attention. Many businesses in Lindisfarne reported a brisk trade from tourists who had come to observe the two gladiators. The Sotol Saloon, of course, was a major beneficiary, but Hubschrauber's General Store across the street turned the Sanchez-Hamaker Gunfight into a gold mine. Betsy Hubschrauber correctly foresaw that the drama of the prolonged confrontation between the two lean, angry cowboys would appeal irresistibly to tens, perhaps hundreds of thousands of hero-hungry Americans. She commissioned the Kalplish Ranch foreman, Miguel Cervantes, who dabbled in sculpture, to produce small statues of Randall and Cesar. Within six weeks after the fight began, she was selling, as fast as they could be produced, crude plaster replicas of the two men. Betsy, who was now decked out in dresses and bonnets with more and larger bows on them than ever, also sold various postcards with photographs of the two men, of the toxboxes and box holsters, and of the entire scene. It was rumored that,

when the gunfight reached its deadly conclusion, she had a storeroom packed full of bogus postcards which had been secretly made by a photographer using models. They showed either man sprawled in the street dead of gory bullet wounds.

(Continued: See SIX-GUN III)

RODEO

"This is our harvest," Oliver Merton told a *New York Times* reporter during the Merton Ranch rodeo in 1886. They were sitting atop the famous twelve-pole-high, twelve-sided Merton corral. "All the constructs of our lonely desert days come to fruition during our rodeos, or roundups, as some people call them."

"You must be in considerable suspense as you wait to find out what your profit or loss is," the reporter said.

"Idiot." Merton climbed down and stalked away.

The reporter filed a story about arrogant Texas Occident ranchers in the Lindisfarne telegraph office the next day. Then he boarded a Houston-bound train, never to return.

What Merton was referring to was the concern with form and order which, beginning in the late 1870's, had increasingly captured the imagination of the cowboys and ranchers in the Occident, and which had begun on the very spot where Merton and the reporter parted company. Credit is generally given to Miguel Cervantes, the foreman of the Kalplish Ranch who, with his crew, was helping out during the 1878 Merton rodeo (from Spanish *rodear*, "to surround"), for making the simple observation that would lead to the opening of many doors in many minds.

A runaway yearling named Anastasia, however, also deserves part of the credit. A brindle-colored heifer with a single stub horn, Anastasia was destined to become the grandmother of Pickup, the ranch's best-known cow, but on the day in question she was interested only in escaping the Merton corral. Foaming at the mouth, her tail flying, she dodged the loop of a cowboy's lariat and raced around the circular pen, evaded another cowboy by darting across to the other side, evaded still another, ran to the center of the arena, spun, thundered toward the fence again, and leaped, knocking off the top two boards as she scrambled over.

"Son of a bitch!" several cowboys swore; Miguel Cervantes, however, paid no attention to the multi-colored yearling as she galloped away toward Ordnance Butte with Alfonso Vela chasing her. Instead, Miguel paced around the interior of the old corral, clucking his tongue thoughtfully. When he had walked a full circle, he stopped, regarded the center of the pen, and began pointing at first one place on the fence, then another.

"What in the hell are you doing, Miguel?" Merton yelled.

"She made a full circle as of right here," Miguel said without looking up. "Then—" bending at times to ascertain Anastasia's tracks, he walked straight across to the other side as Merton fell in step with him. When he reached the opposite fence he turned and nodded. "Exactly bisecting the center. She ran a diameter."

"What? What?" Merton shook Miguel's shoulder. "What are you saying?"

Miguel turned left. "Then she ran with the fence, on the circle—" he walked rapidly, becoming more and more agitated—"on the circle, making an arc to here, and then straight to get past Alfonso, to another point at the fence; that's a chord."

Merton was catching Miguel's excitement by then, and most of the cowboys had crowded in behind them. Merton said. "Yes! A chord, that's right. Then what?"

"Along the fence." Miguel walked rapidly. "Here she went toward the center again—" they followed the tracks breathlessly—"and at dead center—"

"A radius!" Merton said.

"A radius. And she spun at dead center and raced along the—"

"The diameter she had made earlier." Merton bent to study the tracks, his hands on his knees. "And followed that bisection, and then she jumped."

"Right." Miguel sighed deeply, straightened, and smiled. Some of the cowboys shook their heads in wonder, while others edged away uneasily and cut themselves a chew of tobacco.

"I suppose it was an affirmation for all of us," Miguel was to write to a friend that winter. "Something we had all suspected, or known, or wanted to know, that in the apparent chaos of daily events—of riding endless miles over terrain shaped only by the earth's eruptive turmoil and the cutting wind and flash flood; of seeing the eagle-torn lamb and lion-killed colt; of burning brush, hammering staples, pursuing animals, always pursuing—that there was an underlying order to all of it that was crisp, simple, and beautiful. That there was geometry. And a beast had to show us; that was crucial. A beast had to trace circle, chord, arc, radius, and diameter, had to show us in the seeming lawlessness of natural law that single body of laws in which letter and spirit are eternally one and the same."

There were detractors in later years, allbeit few and never vociferous, who alleged that Anastasia ran a circle because the corral had been built in a circle, that to get from one side of the corral to the other she would of necessity have to run a chord or diameter, and that her returning to the exact center was sheer coincidence: after all, if a cow is to escape from a pen, she has to be at some point inside it, and that point might as well be the center as not. No real opposition, however, ever developed to the movement that began in the Merton corral.

Work was halted often and at length for the rest of that day, and on every day to come of the Merton rodeo, as first one cowboy, then another began to perceive what, Miguel wrote later, "We all wept that we had not perceived years ago." When Ralph Garza and Rudolfo Miller roped a calf and others threw it to the ground for brand-painting, for example, Hurley Perkins, the Kalplish Ranch wrangler, leaped from his horse and raced toward the calf, shouting for the men to stop.

"Look," Hurley said as he stood over the calf, pointing from one taut lariat stretched between saddle horn and calf to the other, "the ropes form the legs of a triangle. The calf is the apex."

"Ah." Miguel joined Hurley by the calf. "And the base is the straight line between Ralph and Rudolfo's horses."

Oliver Merton also joined them. He had been momentarily irritated by yet another interruption of the work but was quickly caught up in their interest. He said, "But what if you extend the lines formed by the converging lariats beyond the apex of the calf, in the opposite directions?" He walked away from the calf in the straight line indicated by Ralph's lariat, and Hurley, understanding him, walked away in the direction of Rudolfo's rope. They stopped at the fence.

"Another triangle," Miguel said.

"But now the new legs you've traced can also form angles—and triangles—on the other sides with the ropes." Ralph said.

Hurley nodded. "Reflex angles."

"What if you imagine all the legs to be infinitely extended?" Miguel asked. "Then all the angles they would form, if you consider them from the calf, would encompass the whole world."

"If you assume that they curve with the earth," Oliver said.

Ralph patted his horse, which had become restive during the delay in brand-painting the calf. "Or, if you consider all the legs to be the same length as the one Hurley walked to the fence, they could be points on a circle."

"Yes," Hurley said. "A circle within a circle."

"Like the orbits of planets?" Rudolfo asked.

"No." Miguel pointed toward the center of the corral. "Anastasia's center is there. So all they share is the point on the circumference where Hurley is."

"Or where I am," Oliver said, a little miffed.

Later that afternoon Rudolfo spotted a trapezoid formed by calves, horses, cowboys, and ropes, and immediately thereafter a parallelogram. The men halted work each time to pace off and recreate the form, some of them standing at the remembered corners with their arms extended in imitation of the angles, others tracing the figure in the dust with their toes. As twilight gathered, several cowboys shouted in unison when

a belligerent two-year-old bull raced along Anastasia's diameter, spun at the center, and charged toward the fence in an exact perpendicular, forming a right angle.

The 1878 Merton rodeo lasted well into December instead of mid-October as Oliver Merton had expected. Each day brought new revelations: ovals, ellipses, bisected rectangles. By late November the cowboys were roping in concerted, intentional geometric patterns, and, as Miguel wrote, "the very animals themselves seemed to apprehend our motives."

On the last day of the rodeo, fittingly, what had not happened at all before occurred again and again: the cowboys' ropes intersected at right angles and in the same lengths, maddened cows crashed into the old corral at equidistant points A-B-C-D, culled steers huddled over and over in perfect right-angled, four- and equal-sided configurations.

"In a word," Miguel wrote, "all things formed squares, formed perfection. We went away from the Merton rodeo wondering at the harmony between the brute, mindless cow and abstract, celestial planes."

Events during the rodeos at the Kalplish and Shumacher ranches the following year served only to intensify that wonderment. Day after day, amid the bawling cattle, the roiling dust, the sweat and exasperation and danger, the men encountered sectors and secants, tangents, rhomboids, and rhombi.

"It was an exhilarating time," Miguel wrote: "but man is not an easily satisfied creature, and no satisfaction is permanent. By the time the rodeos were over in early January, more than one of us had voiced privately a vague malcontent, a suspicion that beyond our pleasure in discovering these plane configurations there lay some even more felicitous revelation. But we could not think what it might be."

The revelation came during the 1880 Merton rodeo from an unexpected source, Numero Herrenmeyer, Ralph Garza's bright, inquisitive sixteen-year-old nephew, who had been allowed to work in the rodeo for the first time that fall. On the second day of the rodeo Ralph, Hurley Perkins, and Rudolfo Miller were dragging roped calves toward the center of the arena. Alfonso Vela was about to brandpaint a calf Numero was helping to hold down when Numero stood up and shouted for Alfonso to stop.

"What?" Alfonso pulled his brush back, watching in disgust as the paint ran down his arm.

"Look." Numero pointed at the struggling, bellowing calf. "One. One calf."

"Si, dammit, of course it's one." Alfonso shouted. "You were expecting four?"

"Not four calves; one calf, but four legs. See? One, four," Numero said.

Oliver Merton and Miguel Cervantes ran across the pen to stop the enraged Alfonso from splattering the paintbrush in Numero's face. "What's going on?" Merton asked.

"This crazy Numero is what's going on. He sees one calf here, and it has four legs. For that I get paint running down to my elbow."

"Not for that in itself," Numero said quickly to Merton. "For the squaring of it, the progression."

Merton shook the boy. "What? What squaring? What progression? What the hell are you talking about?"

"One calf," Numero said, "one squared is one; the one in the many, the many in the one. Then there are four legs; that's two squared."

"One squared, two—" Staring, Merton released him.

"And see!" Numero pointed at his uncle and the other cowboys waiting with three calves behind them. "Three men, three horses, three more calves; that's three squared. That's one, two, and three perfected."

Miguel had pulled the swearing Alfonso a safe distance away from the boy. He said, "And are you thinking of this downed calf, plus the other three waiting, their legs?"

"Sixteen legs. That's four squared," Numero said.

"All of the other cowboys had gathered by then," Miguel wrote later, "for the air fairly prickled with excitement at Numero's observation. Oliver asked the boy for the manifestation of the square of five, but the boy could give him none. And all that afternoon we searched for the square of five, but could not find it."

They searched the next day too, which was Thursday, and Friday and

Saturday also, finding nothing. On Sunday, seeing that the men were exhausted and demoralized, Merton gave them the day off, and he, Miguel, and many others went to the church service in Lindisfarne. There, as the minister began to read in the eighth chapter of Ezekiel, they found not the answer they had been searching for but the reason they should not want to find the answer.

"Oliver had nodded off, if the truth be told," Miguel wrote; "but as the preacher read about the evils which Ezekiel saw in his vision, Oliver roused up, frowned deeply, and leaned forward, listening to the preacher intensely. At first I could not understand why, but then I too remembered in the sixteenth verse of Ezekiel the men committing the worst abominations of all, and the number of them, and as the preacher intoned 'five and twenty men with their backs toward the temple,' I leaped up with Oliver, both of us shouting, 'That's it!' and to the astonishment of the preacher and his congregation we led our men out of the church and headed back to the ranch, for we knew that we had not been able to find any fives or squares of five because it was the forbidden number, the number of the five senses, of the twenty-five wicked counselors in Ezekiel 11, and of the five evil kings of Midian in the book of Numbers."

They returned to work, explaining to the men that they should forget about fives. Immediately other squares began to appear; Hurley Perkins ran thirty-six calves, six squared, that is, into the holding pen and had barely counted them before Rudolfo added thirteen more to make the square of seven, and Numero and Ralph chased in another thirty-two to make eighty-one, or nine squared. Their faith reestablished, the men worked without interruption until well past sundown, sure that sixty-four, or eight squared, would appear. But as they turned the last calf loose, their hopes dimmed, and their spirits drooped.

"I'll be dogged," Oliver said, finishing his tally sheets. "You know how many steers we worked today? Thirty-six."

"We already had a six squared." Numero muttered.

Merton added, "And sixty-four heifers."

"Eight squared!" a dozen voices shouted.

Young Numero, his voice shaking, cried, "And thirty-six plus sixty-four is a hundred. Ten squared!"

"Perfection perfected," Miguel whispered, and memories of the Merton rodeo of 1880 have not dimmed in the Texas Occident to the present day.

"We know we have reached the limit of plane figures, and that squaring too must soon become repetitious," Miguel wrote to a friend when the rodeo had finished in mid-February. "We are ready now for three-dimensional figures, for cubes and solids, sure they will come, not knowing when or how."

They came on October 20 two years later, on the first day of the Shumacher Ranch rodeo. The same Numero Herrenmeyer, whom Arturo Shumacher I had hired away from the Merton Ranch the previous year, make the breakthrough shortly after sunup as the first batch of heifers was driven into a catchpen.

"Look," Numero said to Arturo, "eight heifers."

"Don't start that," Arturo replied. "We're all tired of squares."

"Eight isn't a square; it's a cube. Two times two times two."

Arturo stared at Numero as the Shumacher foreman, Valentine Finch, drove eight more heifers into the pen. "A cube—"

"And now there are sixteen," Numero said.

Arturo held up his hand, "I *know* sixteen's a square. So don't —"

"But sixteen calves have sixty-four legs," Numero said; "that's four cubed."

When they gathered around the chuckwagon at noon, many of the cowboys speculated about Numero's discoveries, sure that others would follow quickly. Valentine Finch, however, shook his head worriedly. "We skipped three cubed. I don't like that."

Arturo, who had been seated on a flat boulder some distance away while he wrote in his account book, rejoined the men after putting the book in his saddlebag. "Twenty-seven of us, counting the cook," he said to Finch.

Numero smiled, "Three cubed."

By sundown they had brand-painted 216 head of cattle, which Numero recognized as six cubed, and at the end of four weeks they drove 512 steers (eight cubed) to the shipping yards in Lindisfarne. When the rodeo was finished two months later and the last cow released back on the range, Arturo made his final notation in his tally book and closed it, saying, "There arc 1,728 head on the home place."

"Twelve cubed," Numero said. Valentine Finch and many of the cowboys nodded with pleasure.

"By then we were not surprised," Miguel Cervantes wrote. "We had learned that all creation was numbered, ourselves included, and numbered harmoniously. We welcomed these new evidences of proportion and balance with open arms."

The numerical leap to abstract solids accomplished, the cowboys of the Occident wasted little time at the next rodeo on the Kalplish Ranch in moving on to concrete manifestations.

"That was a simple transferral," Miguel wrote. "Diameters were cut across corrals, we saw, by cows of flesh, bone, hair, and sinew, of height, width, length, and weight. We no longer perceived chords and perpendiculars as concepts, as theoretical measures and boundaries; we saw them as wild-eyed, foaming trajectories, as hurtling, bellowing, colliding bodies, as life. And when we pause now, we pause to recapitulate not just angle and arc but mass, momentum, and fury of the angle-shaper, the thunder of its hooves and shudder of the ground, the burnish of its mottled back and glint of its horns in the slant autumn sun. We pause to savor not only form but the stuff of form."

Attention to color and sound, in fact, so dominated the 1884 Merton rodeo that it lasted from early October until the following April, and the Kalplish and Shumacher rodeos of 1885 and 1886 scarcely finished before the next year's began. Ironically, the rodeo at which the New York reporter became offended was the last true ranch rodeo held in the Occident, for when it ended in August, 1887, Oliver Merton called a meeting of the Kalplish and Shumacher crews as well as all the other ranch crews in the Occident to propose an alternative rodeo.

"Regrettably, we must find a way to divide our work from our more important pursuits, our aesthetic interests," Merton stated in his introductory remarks as he stood in the center of his twelve-sided main corral, built in 1884 of twelve-vara-long lodgepole pines shipped in from Montana, twelve logs high, with twelve gates. "Therefore, I propose we hold an annual rodeo at which we may indulge our interests in geometry, still and moving form, spectra, and all the other phenomena, and that we make no pretense of work during this time; and that, further, we keep our working rodeos separate from this time, and call them *roundups*."

Merton's proposal was vigorously opposed by many cowboys who agreed with Hurley Perkins that any separation of art and work was akin to separating breath and life, but eventually more practical heads prevailed.

The first Occidental Rodeo was held at an arena built on the outskirts of Lindisfarne and lasted from mid-July to September 1, 1888. To the dismay of pioneers such as Miguel Cervantes, Oliver Merton, and Rudolfo Miller who had seen those first elementary forms in the Merton corral, however, the participants quickly divided into two groups, those with still- and moving-form interests, the still-form adherents delving ever more deeply into every aspect of blend and variation in the color spectrum from rainbows to ocotillo blossoms to potted ferns, and into proportionate form within geometric concepts. The moving-form group, however, soon took what many regarded as a perverse turn, centering less and less on the resultant geometry and form of completed movement and more and more on its instigation, even to the extent of causing unnatural movement by riding mentally unstable horses or emotionally disturbed bulls.

By 1891 the vogue for screaming, bucking horses and bellowing, twisting bulls had captured the limited imaginations of many from outside the Occident, and the founders of the Occidental Rodeo discovered to their consternation that outsiders had pushed in with their deranged, unhappy animals and taken over.

"What do you make of this, Miguel?" a bewildered Oliver Merton asked the Kalplish Ranch foreman on the second day of the 1891 rodeo.

Miguel replied, "All I know is, this is the last time I'm bringing my pied marigolds to any damned rodeo anywhere." And thus was determined the demise of the Texas Occidental Rodeo.

WINDMILLS

The first windmills in the Texas Occident were literally wind-*mills* in which wind-powered machinery was employed in various processing capacities. Advertisements in the Lindisfarne *Weekly Gatherer* from the mid-1880's announce the availability of the Franz Stoneham, Udo Hubschrauber, and Joseph Vinson mills for "pressing yucca fiber, crushing rock to caliche, juicing fruits, and grinding grains of all types." These windmills were of the old Dutch design, the mill being both mill and house. A tail, or vane, caused the whole structure to rotate on its base so that the great sail-wheel always faced into the wind.

Unfortunately these early entrepreneurs did not reckon with the force of the spring winds in the Big Bend area. On March 28, 1887, according to the *Gatherer*, the sail-wheel of the Vinson mill "was lifted off its shaft by ferocious winds, thrown spinning into the sky where a golden eagle accosted it in misguided amorousness and dissolved in a great shower of feathers, and the wheel spun on until it shattered against Elephant Butte."

On April 7 of the same year, the Hubschrauber mill met a worse fate in winds estimated at 110 knots per hour. The *Gatherer* quotes Betsy Hubschrauber, the only surviving member of the family: "The force of the wind grew stronger, and the grindstones did turn faster than ever before. Papa shouted to Ernst to brake the sail-wheel and stop it, and Ernst did set the brake, but the teeth of the cogwheels sheared off like warm butter, the sail-wheel whirled even faster, and the whole mill shook

most oddly. I ran to the door and saw that the mill had risen six or
seven feet off the ground. I leaped, crying to Grandmother and Papa
and Ernst to do likewise, but they heard me not in the turmoil, and
as I lay on the ground, my ankle sprained, the mill rose higher into
the sky, the sail-wheel spinning so fast it was well-nigh invisible, and
the others knew not their plight until they looked out the windows as
they passed over Panther Ridge." A week later the *Gatherer* reported
debris from the mill had been found 200 miles southeast in the Del
Rio area. In the wake of these disasters, Franz Stoneham and other mill
operators closed and dismantled their mills or abandoned them.

The windmill commonly identified with the Texas Occident, that is,
a wheel of oblique metal blades set above a gaunt wood or metal derrick and intended to draw water from a well for cattle, came into use
in the 1890's and was a practical tool on the ranches for two or three
decades. Long before this machine's appearance, however, the selective
breeding programs which were to render it obsolete had been started
on the Shumacher Ranch and other ranches in the area. Shrewd cattlemen had not failed to notice the highly efficient water-retention capa-
bilities which had adapted the javelina so superbly to desert conditions,
and they determined to isolate and develop the same characteristics in
their cattle. Thus by 1915 the hardy Desert Hereford and Bactrian
Hereford varieties had been introduced, the Chihuahuan Shorthorn
appeared in 1919, and in 1921 the Shumacher Ranch announced the
compact, wiry Spiny Angus, which could, Arturo Shumacher III once
claimed, "sustain itself for a week on a few mouthfuls of dry sand, and
would drown in a thick fog."

The Spiny Angus doomed the windmill, or so it seemed. When a
windmill gearbox wore out or a derrick collapsed during the next decade,
the ranchers simply ignored them, for their cattle no longer needed
the water. By 1935 hardly a single windmill wheel was turning in all
of the Texas Occident, and by the end of World War II only three standing derricks were counted in Brewster, Jeff Davis, and Presidio Coun-
ties. An aging rancher on Cabora Creek, Tad Kalplish II, was perhaps

symptomatic of the general indifference: acting on a nostalgic impulse, he bought a new steel windmill and had the crate deposited beside his house, but never drilled a well or erected the derrick.

Just when the total demise of the windmill seemed certain, resistance developed from an unexpected source. Speaking before the Arroyo Art Alliance, the prominent Western artist Ramon Sooguns diverged from his prepared lecture on succulent shadowing with watercolors to shout angrily, "There is only one windmill worth painting left in all of the Texas Occident. Why don't they just drive over our tubes of paint with a steamroller or burn all our easels if they want us to stop painting?"

The alarm sounded, albeit late; various organizations and individual artists joined the struggle to return the windmill. University art departments erected miniature windmills in their studios and encouraged students to substitute windmill-study for life-study courses. A retired high school art teacher single-handedly built a windmill and had it erected in the local schoolyard. Sooguns published a pamphlet at his own expense accusing ranchers of depriving the artist of "the single indispensable element in any Western painting."

Despite the uproar, however, a central—and the only relevant—fact remained: the valleys, slopes, and prairies of the Occident were as devoid of windmills as ever. Soon the movement began to lose momentum, and had it not been for an editorial by Monahans Macleoud, editor of the *Gatherer*, Occidental Texas would have been windmillless to the present day. "I saw a painting by Ramon Sooguns at an opening in a Houston gallery a few days hence," Macleoud wrote; "the craggy sentinel rimrocks of the Davis Mountains leaned ominously over the scene. Indians bent their bows at galloping, frothing buffalo. A cowboy was suspended in mid-air over a rearing horse gored by a longhorn. A panther lunged at a new-born calf whose brave, still-weak mother set herself to meet fang and claws. Liveoak, mesquite, eagle, vulture, roadrunner, antelope, and jackrabbit denizened the canvas, yet for me it was empty as Dry Creek in a drought, colorless, depthless, and meaningless. 'Where are the windmills?' I asked, turning to Sooguns. 'How can you call this

a painting unless there is a windmill?' And Sooguns replied, 'How can I paint what is not there? I want the windmill even more than you, but it is not there. Go home and see for yourself.' "

Macleoud ended with a stirring plea for action that was heeded by one of his few subscribers, Tad Kalplish II. Recalling the warped, mud-dobber-filled crate beside his house, Kalplish called in all the available ranchhands and set them to work assembling the new but rusted windmill near the main entrance to the Cabora Creek headquarters that same afternoon. When one of the cowboys complained, "They ain't even a well there," he replied, "The hell with the well. That's not the point."

So the gesture was made that quickly was copied; soon windwheels were whirling once again on derricks from Sierra Blanca to Sanderson, from Guadalupe Pass to the Christmas Mountains, operating non-existent pumps in undrilled wells, raising non-existent water for cows that didn't drink, and the western artist was whole again.

KNOBITY

(Note: The following narration, believed to be the first written documentation of Texas Occidental knobity, was discovered in the study of the well-known historian Prof. Sweetwater Davis by his wife shortly after his mysterious disappearance in 1984. Professor Davis was said to have returned from an abbreviated trip to the Texas Occident just before he disappeared.)

I had called from Dallas to ask Tad Kalplish III, the Princeton-educated, octogenarian son and grandson of pioneer Texas Occident ranchers, if he knew anything about the old Comanche war trails crossing Cabora Creek north of the Rio Grande.

"I can show you the Coyote-Eye and Bluefeather trails. They run for thirty miles across the ranch," he said. He offered to pick me up at the Midland airport on his way back from Abilene, where he also had ranching interests.

Kalplish waved off my attempts to thank him when I met him at the airport, saying, "It's a long, lonely drive down to Lindisfarne; I'm happy for the company." Below average height even in his boots, he was a leathery eighty-two years old, white-haired, with a bushy, tobacco-stained mustache; his stomach swayed over a thick silver belt buckle, but his shoulders were square in a flowered western shirt, his step quick and sure.

He patted the cooler between us as we got into his Mercedes. "For company; it's nine beers from here to the ranch." As soon as we were headed west toward Pecos on Interstate 20, he opened a Coors, saying,

"I don't like these freeways. You can't talk to a man on them."

"We may be able to talk," I answered.

He shook his head. "Not what I meant." Before I could ask what he did mean, he began talking about the Bluefeather Trail, and for the next hour I scribbled nonstop in my notebook except when he paused to spit in the chamber pot-shaped cuspidor at his feet. Near the Monahans exit he crushed his beer can between large-knuckled hands, dropped it on the floor, and opened a fresh one.

Finally, as we left the freeway at Pecos and turned toward Balmorhea, he said, "My talker's tuckered." He opened a beer and offered me one.

"And I've got writer's cramp." I flexed my arm. "I'm really grateful to you, Mr. Kalplish."

"Not at all." He raised two fingers from the steering wheel as we met a northbound pickup pulling a horse trailer. The other driver, a bearded cowboy, returned the greeting. A few miles later we met a cattle truck with three men wearing Stetsons in the cab, and he lifted one, two, then three fingers, saying, "Ah! Good!"

"I'd forgotten the friendliness of Texas Occident drivers," I said. "It's a fine custom."

He mused a bit, gazing beyond Balmorhea toward the undulating horizon of the Davis Mountains. "Friendliness? Well, yes. The phatic greeting, don't they call it? 'Hello: I'm here, you're here, and we're not going to kill each other.' But it's a good deal more than that."

He hummed and tapped the steering wheel. We met a motor home from Iowa, then a car with Minnesota plates, both of which he ignored, then a double-cab pickup with two large barking dogs in the back. Moving his index finger slowly from side to side, Kalplish exchanged greetings with the gray-haired driver. After we passed, he compressed his lips, closed his eyes, and nodded. "True, Miguel," he said; "true, indeed."

After a few minutes the old man said again, "Friendliness, yes. But a great deal more than that."

"I don't understand."

"It involves loneliness, and the need to alleviate that loneliness." He slowed the car, crushed his beer can, and took another. "In the old days there was loneliness also, but it was not so bad. When the men met on the trail they stopped to talk while their horses grazed and rested. Sometimes they stopped for hours, or even camped for the night right there."

He whacked the car door angrily with the side of his boot. "But automobiles don't graze. They don't need rest. They don't even sweat. And they go too fast to be stopped anyway." He shook his head and was silent while a sleek red Porsche passed us and disappeared over the hill. "Those were dark days, I can tell you, when the lonely men out here first began to understand these things, first saw their friends whizzing by at seventy miles an hour without stopping, with just a quick wave. No wonder knobiters call them the Dark Ages."

"Knobiters?"

"Knob artists. Men that do knobity."

"Knob artists? Knobity?"

"Kindly don't parrot me. *Knobity* is short for 'knob howdy': knobowdy, knobady, knobity. Anybody could see that, seems like."

"I suppose so." I wrote the word in my notebook. "But what's this about knobs?"

"The knob on the steering wheel, of course; we all used to have them, before power steering. That's where the right hand was; that's where it all began. Now don't interrupt me," Kalplish snapped.

"Sorry."

"The Dark Ages. Those were the days of loneliness. And then the Enlightenment began. Some say this man, some say that made the discovery, but most agree it was the Zeitgeist, it was in the air, it had to happen."

He stopped talking as we drove into Balmorhea. His fingers curved, straightened, waggled, literally danced on the steering wheel as we met a Suburban, then a Cadillac. I opened a beer without waiting for an invitation as we left the town and started the long climb to Ft. Davis.

"At first it was primitive." Kalplish gestured toward a boulder-strewn slope on our right. "I remember, clear as I see that windmill up there, the first knobity I ever understood. My father and I were going to Terlingua in our new Pierce-Arrow when we met Oliver Merton in his Model T and he told us—in knobity—there was a herd of wild burros on the road just over the hill. 'Papa,' I yelled, 'did you see what Oliver said? There's burros over the hill.' 'What?' he said; 'Burros? Nonsense!' We sailed over that hill, killed three burros, and scattered the Pierce-Arrow for two hundred yards."

"That's incredible." I stared at him, my notebook forgotten.

"Appreciate it if you don't interrupt," he said irritably. "You need to understand the terrible isolation of desert people to comprehend how rapidly the language increased. Not single meanings, but whole groups of words appeared simultaneously. These highway meetings at combined speeds of 120, 140, 160 miles an hour became moments of acutest communicative intensity."

"I can understand the loneliness," I said; "but communication—"

"It isn't just the loneliness, it's the result of man and his integration with the automobile. Think about two clerks in a store: they work side by side all week long and scarcely notice each other, but on Sunday they meet in their cars and gape, wave, and honk like long-lost brothers. Think about how much more such a meeting means to a man who's just spent six solitary weeks in a line-camp. So the language—"

"Mr. Kalplish—" I was fumbling in the cooler—"Mr. Kalplish, isn't 'language' an exaggeration? You're talking about ten fingers, not the human tongue."

"*Five* fingers. That was a controversy, the objections of the left-handers, and of those who claimed that using both hands would allow us infinite modulation of stress, voice, and tone. But the direct discourse adherents said no: Let it be the right hand. Let it be on the steering wheel, in touch with the road, the power, the very speed that necessitates the moment. Let there be no ornamentation, no use of sun visors or headlights or windshield wipers to modify meaning."

"But fingers are not a tongue—"

"*One* tongue. There are *four* fingers, plus a thumb; each has joints, a nail, a knuckle; each can curl, twirl, bend, wag, touch the other, touch the wheel in a thousand ways, and in infinitely different sequences. It is *language*."

As we rounded a curve we saw a battered green Suburban parked on the shoulder. The driver, a middle-aged, thick-trunked man with a greasy cap set backwards on his head, was standing by the fence. Elbow resting on a post, a beer in his hand, he stared westward into a canyon dark with juniper brush. He did not turn around when Kalplish honked.

"Willy Edel," Kalplish muttered; "I wonder if Herrenmeyer . . . ."

He set his Coors on the dash and took a pinch of Copenhagen. "So the first knobity were just practical. News. And often still are. You remember the cowboy we met just off the freeway?"

"Yes."

"He told me that Beto Dirksen's got new mud flaps. And the three men in the cattle truck? The driver said Carrasco's has Pearl Light on special, fifty cents off." He bent to use the spittoon.

"I see what you mean," I said.

"But the desire to go beyond that was present from the beginning. I remember—it couldn't have been more than six months after Papa hit the burros—I remember Arturo Mendoza's first couplet:

> Many as spines on a cactus
> Are the troubles have racked us."

"Well—" I began.

"I'm not saying it was great." He spat again and got a beer. "I'm saying that was the start, and that it was necessary. I, myself, in my callow youth, did some sentimental love knobity. Never mind who this one was about:

> Before I'd her dishonorably seduce
> I'd gnaw the bark off a creosote bush."

We met a Bronco just then that saved me from having to comment.

Kalplish chuckled fondly after the driver, a pale boy wearing a black, peaked hat with a deep dent in the crown, had passed. "Every generation starts with love. That was young George Vernon Karstetter. Here's what he said:

> How she sighed when I proposed her
> In the cool of the pickup air conditioner."

"Speaking of air conditioners," I said, "they must have increased the alienation out here. Closing the windows—"

He held up his hand for silence, pointing ahead to a pickup that appeared to have stopped suddenly, the rear wheels still on the highway. Two men, their jeans stuffed into knee-high boots, were sitting cross-legged on the caliche, hats on the ground beside them, their hands clasped before them prayerfully. Neither looked at us, and Kalplish did not honk.

"Hmm-hmm!" Kalplish pushed his hat up and scratched his head. "That was Arvil Judson and Jesus Perkins. Herrenmeyer, for certain."

After a minute or two of silence, he said, "You're mistaken about air conditioners; they enhance knobity, because they allowed us to concentrate our powers on one medium. We also feared that television might spell the end, but has it occurred to you how closely a windshield resembles a television screen?"

"Well—"

"Knobiters realized that immediately, and there was a flurry of melodrama, of attempts at pathetic TV humor. But that's past. We've left television behind. Actually, the greatest threat has come from dark-tinted windshields."

We came to Ft. Davis then, and as we passed the old fort before we entered the town, Kalplish said, "For many of us, knobity reaches beyond the esthetic moments themselves. Remember the double-cab pickup with the dogs in it? The driver's my Cabora Creek foreman. Here's what he knobited: 'Yesterday we meant to start the Javelina Ridge roundup, but as Fred and Alphonso were saddling up they became entranced by the blending grays and purples in the shadows under the Chinati peaks, so we put off the roundup until Friday. Where beauty is, beef must wait."

I started to reply, but as we passed the courthouse a man flagged us down with his dingy, wide-brimmed brown hat.

"Howdy, Mr. Kalplish," he said. "You going on toward Marfa? Hook Herrenmeyer's only ten minutes ahead of you, and he's fine-tuned today."

"Ah; I thought so," Kalplish said.

"Who is Hook Herrenmeyer?" I asked as we turned toward Marfa, driving much faster than before.

The old man bent over the wheel as the Mercedes neared a hundred miles an hour. "All I can say is, I wish with all my heart we were coming *from* Marfa right now and meeting Hook Herrenmeyer. I would pay a man with a helicopter a fortune to fly me to Marfa right now."

Hanging on grimly as our tires screamed on a sharp curve, I shouted, "Mr. Kalplish, since you're risking my life as well as your own to catch up with him, it seems to me I have a right to know more about this Herrenmeyer."

He glared at me. "All right. I won't say he is one of the immortals of knobity; he hasn't reached Maury Sutter's level, any more than Sutter has Alberto Vela's. But he is, nevertheless, a knobiter of great versatility and power. I'll try to translate a knobity he did south of Marathon when he was only twelve years old and could barely see over the dash of his father's pickup."

Pausing as if to gather strength, he used the spittoon, then began: "As I bent in the sun's first light to staple a loose strand of barbed wire, an anomaly in that desert place, a distilling and instilling of all the rare moisture, and perhaps of all life itself, since moisture is life, a drop of dew beckoned my careless eye, and in that single, transient globule of water poised on an ivory petal of yucca bloom I saw a prismed, prisoned universe caged by writhing ocotillo tendrils—limboed, living cell bars, guarded over by a vast, vigilant, flaggy-winged vulture, sealed beneath by an ivory floor—and the orb of water was as an eye, and the eye was mine, and was also the unbearably immured eye of all things; and I looked

away, crying, 'Are we free? What is free? What is the arching sky but
azure ocotillo bars, what this sphere of earth but a drop of jailing water
in the desert of deserts?' "

Winded, Kalplish tugged a large blue bandanna from his pocket and
dabbed at his eyes. We had slowed to normal speed as he recited.

"Twelve years old," I said. "That's amazing. What about these others?
Can you give examples of Sutter and Vela's work?"

He shot a look of scorn at me. "No one could translate Sutter or Vela,
or even the mature Herrenmeyer."

He braked suddenly as we topped a low hill. Ahead of us a pickup
was stopped diagonally in the middle of the road, fresh skid marks end-
ing at its tires. Smoke puffed from the tailpipe. Two well-dressed men,
apparently ranchers, sat huddled on the pavement, their arms crossed
over their heads as if they were in a hailstorm. A tall young cowboy
was banging his forehead against the tailgate. As we edged by, I saw that
the ranchers were crying unashamedly. The cowboy crumpled to the
pavement, unconscious.

"And that," Kalplish said softly as we gathered speed again, "that is
what Hook Herrenmeyer can do."

We drove in silence for about ten miles. As we neared Marfa, I said,
"Mr. Kalplish, where can I find these other men you mentioned? Sutter and Vela?"

"Who can say? They are where their minds are, where their art is."

"If you don't mind," I said, "I think I'll stay in Marfa instead of going
on to your ranch. I'm going to catch a bus, go home, and get my pickup."

He handed me a beer from the cooler. "Coming back?"

"Yes, sir."

He smiled sadly. "It's a lonely trail out here."

"Mr. Kalplish," I said, "isn't art always so?"

Flexing his fingers, he began to tap the steering wheel as a dust-covered
Suburban loomed up ahead of us. "It's always so, Son."

SIX-GUN III
The Stubbornness of Two Men

While Randall Sanchez and Cesar Hamaker remained crouched in the street, their hands hovering ominously over their box holsters, time crept by with agonizing slowness. October, November, and most of December passed with no word from either Augustus Kalplish, who was searching for Cal Clinnjin, who had stolen Randall's pants with Cesar's toxbox keys in them, or from Leticia Harnsgartner's mother, who was searching for her profligate son, Amos, who had Randall's keys.

On Christmas morning a rare snowstorm surprised Lindisfarne. Busy with present-opening and family gatherings, no one thought of the two men crouched in the street until nearly noon when Betsy Hubschrauber glanced down from her living quarters over her store and saw them. Perhaps she was grateful for their role in her new prosperity, or conscious that Randall's left boot was rotting out because of her errant rainspout; or she may have been simply filled with the Christmas spirit. At any rate, an uncharacteristic wave of guilt and remorse washed over her, and, throwing on a poncho, she grabbed a broom, ran downstairs, and swept the snow off the two men, apologizing for her and the other townspeople's indifference.

"It's Christmas, you know," she said, thumping Randall's hat brim against her knee to break off the icicles, then putting it back on his head. "Folks most likely forgot about you in all the excitement."

"Is it Christmas?" Randall frowned. "Be durn. I lost track." He shouted, "Cesar! Did you know it was Christmas? Merry Christmas!"

"Merry Christmas to you too, Randall," Cesar answered.

The moment of enchantment may have occurred then for Betsy Hub-schrauber; it may have been then that she learned to love Randall San-chez for the dirt crusted on his face, the snow drifted over his brows, the straw, feathers, and scraps of paper trapped in his beard, or the patient resolve in his brown eyes. Or it may have been the culmination of the many times she glimpsed him from her prospering store, which now took up more than half the block and had the largest display windows in Lindisfarne. For whatever reasons, she fell in love with him, and in so doing allied herself with fate for a second time to affect the outcome of a gunfight in Lindisfarne.

On New Year's Day, 1874, a telegram came for Leticia. Her mother, now wholly bedridden, had uncovered evidence of Amos's bacchanalian adventures in the Bahamas, but he had moved on to Havana before her arrival. Bed and all, she had followed him to Cuba, where his riotous-ness had astounded the citizenry, and from there to Haiti, and then to Puerto Rico. He was believed to be headed toward Jamaica, and Leticia's mother, although she had twice been given last rites, was already enroute, firmly believing that she was coming closer to her profligate son, and Randall Sanchez's toxbox keys, with every passing hour.

In the meantime two incidents took place near Lindisfarne in which, according to the *Weekly Gatherer*, "Poetic justice truly triumphed, and two evil men—psychopaths by anyone's definition, and utter sociopaths by the lofty standards of our advanced civilization in the Texas Occident—received their just deserts for actions in stark and instructive contrast to that humane and honorable example being set by those gentlemen Randall Sanchez and Cesar Hamaker, who wait with disciplined patience to kill each in front of Hubschrauber's General Store, where yellow onions may be had this week for thirty-five cents the bushel."

The first incident involved Arch Tawnhoser, a suspected buffalo poacher, who had signed on with the Kalplish Ranch during brandpaint-ing season the previous year but, finding the work too onerous, had quit after a few days. Somehow, he had conceived a bitter grudge against

Tad Kalplish I, and he had spent the fall and winter months preparing his revenge. Stealing a Gatling gun from the Army post at Ft. Davis, he adapted the murderous device to a swivel hip holster in his hideout near Mala Vista on the Rio Grande. He drank heavily in a Mala Vista saloon on the night of February 10, bragging that it would not be long before, compared to Tad Kalplish I, chopped liver would look like angel food cake. Early the next day, witnesses saw him riding in the general direction of the Kalplish Ranch headquarters, still drinking, the Gatling gun strapped to his hip. As he crossed Cabora Creek at midday, however, he fell off his horse and, trapped under the gun, drowned in three inches of water.

In the other incident, Villalobos Smith, a cattle rustler who was widely regarded as having a bright future, devised an elaborate scheme to bushwhack Dangerous Dirk McDougal, his major area rival in the rustling business. With the help of a renegade Kansas dentist, Smith implanted a sawed-off shotgun in the mouth of his horse, Avalanche, an animal well-known for his broad and tasteless sense of humor. The gun was triggered by pulling the horse's head up with the reins. Unfortunately for Smith, on St. Patrick's Day he told his gang members a coarse, shopworn joke about an Irish nun. Not one of the men cracked a smile, but Avalanche threw back his head to laugh, and Smith was killed by his own dastardly invention.

In early April, Leticia's mother telegraphed that she had found nothing in her search for her son, and for Randall Sanchez's toxbox keys. She had followed Amos to Jamaica, where he had spent money wildly in Kingston, but then he had simply disappeared. She intended to follow up the most likely-seeming of the many vague rumors she had heard, traveling to Grenada; if she turned up nothing there, on to Honduras, and then to Panama. She was running low on funds, however, and she was forced to wait in Kingston, her hospital bed having been seized for debt, while her house and her much-coveted whatnot collection were being auctioned off back in Hartford, Connecticut.

(Continued: see SIX-GUN IV)

HORSE-TRAILING

The horse trailer is generally recognized in the Texas Occident as the greatest labor-saving device of the twentieth century.

Before the advent of the horse trailer, horses were transported by hand, the prevailing opinion being that "twelve stout men, neither lame nor lazy," were necessary to carry a horse of average weight over long distances, assuming it was not given to struggling or kicking. Ten men carried at all times; the eleventh commanded and guided, and the twelfth, in rotation, rested.

Horse-bearers used three very different techniques, and each had its adherents. Least popular was the practice by which the legs were securely tied and the horse then hoisted to the men's shoulders like, one disgusted citizen complained in the Lindisfarne *Weekly Gatherer*, "a sack of cottonseed." Although the "bound and determined" method was acknowledged to be safest, many argued that it robbed the horse of its inherent dignity and nobility, traits which were, after all, the spirit and sinew of horse-trailing in the first place. Most preferred the "Trojan Horse" technique in theory, while simultaneously acknowledging its extreme danger since the bearers, three at each front leg and two at each rear leg, raised the horse "straight up, its royal neck nobly arched, its slender legs unfettered as nature itself," one enthralled visitor noted in his journal. The question of which was worse—the heavier front bearing positions, or the more dangerous rear—was raised in every saloon discussion, and never resolved.

A third method utilized a strong, hammock-like fabric woven of yucca fiber and fastened to a sturdy frame. Although Spirithoof, the Merton Ranch's well-known flaghorse for over twenty years, stood with her legs spread in the swaying sling, her nostrils flaring, most horses were borne with their feet skyward, neighing and thrashing, thus originating the saying, "I've got my horse in a sling."

Whatever the method, the ranchers of the Texas Occident were, on the whole, a plain-living, no-frills lot, so an ordinary trip to town required only one horse and twelve men; thus the expression "one-horse town." If a rancher were to visit Ft. Worth or Houston, however, he might lead a caravan of twenty trailing horses and 240 bearers.

In the labor-intensive economy of the mid-nineteenth century, horse-trailing was not an expensive custom for most ranchers. As the century drew to a close and the sweat of the laborer's brow began to cost more, however, many people began to cut corners, first by purchasing light-framed pinto horses which could be carried by fewer men, and later by importing Shetland ponies. Some even resorted to burros. Rancher Tad Kalplish II reportedly made $45,000 in stud fees in a single year with his famed Shetland stallion "Chiquito King," which stood no taller than a good-sized collie.

Many people objected vigorously to these trends. "This reeks of the most blatant parsimony," Marie Macleoud Shumacher, the wildly beautiful young wife of the prominent rancher Arturo II, wrote in a letter to the *Weekly Gatherer*, "and I for one will never stoop to such meanness." She not only made good her promise but improved on it: on Easter Sunday 1888 the Shumachers arrived at the Lindisfarne Methodist Church ahead of a Trojan Horse retinue of fifteen magnificent Clydesdales, "every one as big as an elephant, and every one larger than the last," the society editor of the *Weekly Gatherer* reported. Each was held aloft by twenty-four groaning men.

"Surely," the same writer gushed, "it was horse-trailing's finest hour."

The Shumachers continued their Sunday extravaganza until the Spanish-American War, when Arturo went east to join the national horse-trailing protest against the Rough Riders and Marie could not find enough bearers at any price. Horse-trailing enthusiasts in the Lindisfarne area became demoralized, and a younger, cost-conscious generation, while sorrowing to see the tradition pass, talked openly of its demise. In July 1901 the *Weekly Gatherer* reported, "scarcely a dozen horses are now seen carried down our streets in a week."

The advent of the automobile seemed to solve the problem. Since some ranchers had begun to haul their cattle and sheep to market in stock trucks, it was suggested that horses as well might be transported in this way. A few ranchers, in fact, actually appeared in Lindisfarne in 1909 with their horses tethered in their trucks.

What had appeared to be a solution, however, resulted in a far worse problem, for an outcry against this practice arose immediately. One early opponent wrote in the *Weekly Gatherer*, "To put a horse—a *horse!*— in a rolling prison intended for common cows, or worse, goats, or, God forbid, sheep! Say even that the enclosure had been first thoroughly cleansed of the manure and stench of its previous occupants; the practice is beyond belief, is surely beyond the human capacity for indecency."

In answer to these protests, Lindisfarne blacksmiths crafted a trailer designed solely for horses. A social crisis was averted, and the mechanical horse trailer saved horse-trailing for the generations to come.

An avid horse-trailing enthusiast wrote in the *Gatherer* in 1963, "There is nothing quite so beautiful as a noble horse racing across the harsh and relentless desert at eighty-five miles an hour in a trailer with the top thrown back. His graceful neck is arched, his trembling nostrils flared, his mane and tail flung to the wind like silver filaments or golden tendrils, his amber-tinted highway goggles reflecting the midday sun, his chrome-plated helmet sparkling like a diamond, his long silk scarf undulating gallantly. The sixteen speakers of his sound system caress him with the strains of Debussy, or uplift his heart with some stirring polonaise. Small wonder that he smiles with pleasure, that he laughs aloud with delight when he meets another horse in another trailer whose owner has also taken him out for a two- or three-hundred-mile spin on a splendorous day! What greater satisfaction than to contemplate our marvelous modern trailers, long as pullman cars, decorated with revolutionary slogans or bright murals depicting the trials of migratory laborers? What greater pleasure than to know our beloved horses are surrounded by the utmost in carpeted, insulated, air-conditioned, piped-music comfort? What greater comfort than to think of our horses visiting the skyscraper-canyoned avenues of New York, the lofty peaks of Colorado, the gentle countryside of New England with no danger of bruising their dainty hooves on the unyielding concrete or soiling them on the unhygienic ground?"

The tradition has become ever more popular in the twentieth century. The practice has spread through the middle and even lower classes, until today no one in the Texas Occident would think of going to church or even shopping for groceries without trailing at least one horse behind him.

COWBOY HATS

Few articles of apparel have had more misinformation written about them than the western hat. Since it was called (by writers who had never seen one) the ten-gallon hat, many assumed it was used for water storage, and accounts were written by otherwise rational men about cowboys who lived on hatwater for months at a time and took leisurely hatbaths once a week. The cowboy hat, it was reported, was used to sleep in, like a nest, or to sled down wintry slopes, or to skid sacks of flour. Its broad brim was said to protect cowboys from rain and snow so effectively that a New York newspaper spuriously quoted a rancher as saying, "We wouldn't have a desert out here if they'd stop wearing those damned hats."

The cowboy's love of his hat and reluctance to remove it were legendary. While attending a funeral in Langtry, Texas, Roscoe Judson supposedly refused to take off his hat until two friends upended an empty whisky barrel and lowered it over him so no one could see his shame. Coy Hamaker, meeting a woman on an Ogallala street after a four-year cattle drive, was said to have wrenched his neck so severely while trying to remove his hat that he later died. A Dallas newspaper reported a claim by the prominent Texas Occident rancher's wife Marie Shumacher, never averse to publicity, that her son Arturo III refused to be born until a hat was placed on his head.

For nearly a century, the Eastern press believed that the sole use of the cowboy hat was to lure Indian arrows and bullets. Purported eyewitness accounts told of entire nations of Indian warriors waiting until a cowboy raised his hat on a stick above his head, then expending all their arrows and cartridges, hurling their lances, tomahawks, and every available stone, and going home satisfied. Wells Fargo riders were said to be identified by the ragged bullet holes and crisscrossed arrows in their hats. No matter how sweat-lathered his horse when he galloped up to the way station, a rider's pouch was burned on the spot if his hat was unscarred.

Cowboy hats were thought to be the hiding places of secret messages, maps, ore samples, deeds to ranching empires, packets of love letters, locks of hair, jewelry, cedar chests belonging to long-dead sweethearts, derringers, sawed-off shotguns, Bibles and concordances, bedrolls, and sticks of dynamite. A story persists of a cowboy known only as Rancid Bill whose mother, when she was on her deathbed, gave him five pounds of butter which he carried in his hat for years until, after he had refused numerous requests to remove it, fellow drovers hanged him on the Chisholm Trail a few miles north of the Red River.

Sworn affidavits attest that the petite and beautiful Lupita Nell Slape cowered for thirty-six hours under her lover Hurley Perkins's hat on the floor by a table in the Sotol Saloon in Lindisfarne, Texas, while Hurley pretended to be engaged in a marathon poker game, and while Lupita's seven enraged brothers, barefoot and armed with ten-gauge shotguns, stalked the town. Some historians have claimed that the names of the Perkins children—Crease, Crown, Band, Straw, Felt, Resistol, and Brim— lend further credence to the story.

The media, particularly filmmakers, never bothered to find out what cowboys really wore on their heads. Instead, they altered the shape of the hat again and again to suit America's needs. Silent movies, for example, depicted the front brim of the pony express rider's hat as flattened against the crown by the rider's perpetual speed, thus symbolizing the nation's frenzied westward sprawl. During the Great Depression, movie cowboys wore hats with the crowns eaten away and holes gnawed in the brims, symbolizing the desperate poverty of the time. The villain was often caught sneaking a greedy bite from another man's hat, particularly if it was white.

Movies of the 1940's had pristine heroes with perfect table manners. They knocked out armies of glass-jawed thugs without missing a note in their ballads. They used their six-shooters as stun-guns, administering bloodless, humane concussions by dropping chandeliers on bank robbers' heads or paralyzing murderers' wrists by shooting their weapons out of their hands. The hats worn by Roy Rogers and Gene Autry were designed by Sunday School classes, the crown rising optimistically to the front like a cathedral, the brim curling forward as innocently as a baby's curls.

The Fifties brought the aggressively-jawed rake whose aquiline nose was shadowed by the dipping, sinister beak of his hat, the brim curving back, up, and out like the wings of a predatory bird. No woman from twelve to ninety could hope to save her honor from such a man, and many were reduced to drooling slaves just by seeing his hat.

Variations of this pattern included the low, flat crown with a Valentine-heart crease in the top. This hat was worn by a glib, grinning daredevil whose horse threw him into a haybaler at the climax of the movie, leaving his shattered sweetheart no choice but to marry the molasses-brained sodbuster back in Drone Valley. A filthy hat with a ragged brim hiding all the face but a dangling cigarette stub indicated a deep, putty-hearted thinker who killed two or three extremely evil men a day not for the bounty but because frivolous Chance kept dropping them in his gunsights just when he had decided to become a notary public. The Oscar-winning film *Gloryfelt* starred a hat whose brim swept up over the crown with such dramatic ferocity that it made every heart dream of deeds of boundless valor. Standing-room-only audiences gaped at closeups of the hat on a kitchen table, low-angle shots of it hanging on a wooden peg, teary out-of-focus shots by a rushing waterfall, and ground-level shots panning inexorably toward it in the dust of a lonely street. Finally, as it rested, harsh and inevitable, atop a frilly lavender bedspread, a zoom lens closed in nearer, ever nearer until the hat engulfed screen and screaming viewers and all else.

Movies echoed the prosperity of the early Sixties with the conserva-
tively gray, narrow-brimmed rancher's hat, the parallel ridges on its carefully blocked crown symbolizing the twin virtues of prudence and
ostentation. So staid was this hat that governors, certified public accoun-
tants, and ministers who had never seen horse or cow gladly wore it,
feeling they had bridged the gap between the perils of the wild west
and the safety of the country club. The times changed, however, and
the turbulence of the late Sixties was quickly reflected in the strange,
unlikely shapes of cowboy headgear: huge domed crowns resembling
dunce caps, grain elevators, eggplants, or obese question marks mocked
the shape of man's head—and therefore his heart and soul—and
challenged his values. Hatbands, widening and brightening like rainbows, were made of exotic snakeskins, linked coins, or costly fur; brilli-
ant feathers sprouted from them, and flags, flowers, and streamers too;
caroling parakeets vied for space around the crown with peace symbols.

So the charade has continued, decade after decade. As satellite dishes
brought television, and therefore old western movies, to remote areas
of the Texas Occident, cowboys shook their heads in amusement and
bewilderment at what the world thought they wore.

In 1979 a dramatic breakthrough and reversal nearly occurred during
the state convention of the Spiny Angus Association in San Antonio
when, at the request of many cattlemen, the rancher Tad Kalplish III
addressed the problem in his keynote speech. "I suppose no great harm
has been done," he said. "Still, if you value the truth, and we do value
it in the Texas Occident, you would like to have the record set straight.
And the fact is that no movie ever produced has accurately rendered
the headgear of the working cowboy."

The producer-director Harlan Lionelish, the only man there wearing
a Stetson (in fact, the only man wearing a hat at all), was in the audience
that day, searching for a new approach for his next western film. He
thought he had found it when he heard Kalplish, and after the speech
he quickly cornered the aging rancher, who was being helped from the
stage by Madison Macleoud, editor of the Lindisfarne *Weekly Gatherer*,

grandson of the pioneer bootmaker Angus Macleoud, and son of Monahans Macleoud, who had also edited the *Gatherer*.

"What do cowboys really wear?" Lionelish asked, his pen ready over a notepad.

"Why, what anybody wears," Kalplish replied. "At a typical roundup I suppose the most likely hat to be seen is the standard conservative, stiff, narrow-brimmed bowler, or derby hat, not one whit different from what you'd see in the London financial district."

"Bowler." Lionelish stared at the old man, tapping his pen on the notepad.

Macleoud said, "People think cowboys all wear the same kind of hat, like a uniform, but that's not so. They're individuals, just like everyone else."

"Right," Kalplish said; "unless you count the hornhat decade."

Lionelish frowned. "Hornhat?"

"Like the Vikings wore. It seemed to make sense when it started. People liked the symbolism. The old long horns were wild and romantic looking, and they represented our way of life. They were attached to a kind of skullcap that looked a lot like the old leather football helmets, with a chin strap. Funny how stubborn people can be. Right from the start, everybody saw how impractical they were—some of them were eight feet from tip to tip—but they still lasted from 1910 to 1922. There were woundings and even accidental deaths when men turned their heads too quickly; I've seen a dozen friends drop to the ground when someone shouted to a man wearing a hornhat. Seagraves Judson gored his favorite horse right beside the bunkhouse. Miguel Cervantes would have died hanging between two live oaks if some picnickers hadn't come along."

Kalplish gazed at the Spiny Angus banner overhead for a moment and brushed away a tear. "My own mother went home to her kinfolks in East Texas and never returned because of Tad II's hornhat. He heard a shot outside—it was Seagraves killing a rattlesnake—and before he thought, he'd smashed two big vases and rent an antique Norman tapestry from side to side."

"The new Shorthorn breed didn't help?" Macleoud asked.

"When it stopped, it stopped. A few men tried the shorter horns, but hornhats were finished." Kalplish shook his head. "Kind of a shame."

Lionelish had taken no notes. He said, "So now they wear—"

"Sometimes they don't wear hats. All this claptrap about the sun baking brains, needle-sharp sleet, and hailstones big as armadillos, you know, is foolishness. Beto Dirksen generally wears a hairnet. Rayferd Valenzuela used to wear a skimmer. Arvil Judson and—"

"Hairnet," Lionelish said.

"Arvil Judson and Jesus Perkins have worn berets for years, all their lives I guess, just like their dads did." Kalplish chuckled as he put on his tweed touring cap. "Arvil wore a beanie for a couple of years, though, and then a skullcap for a while."

"Berets. Beanie."

While Kalplish went on talking a bit absent-mindedly about Lilburn Glazebrook's fez and Rudolpho Heffel's pith helmet, Lionelish spun on his heel, strode to the bar, started to order a drink, changed his mind, and left the premises.

"Why, where is that fellow?" Kalplish asked Macleoud, surprised.

"I believe he's gone, Tad," Macleoud said.

The old rancher shook his head wearily. "Well, I suppose the world never will know any different."

And until now, it hasn't.

SPURS

Historians of the Texas Occident have gradually begun to realize that some of the more baffling aspects of the cowboy's complex personality are related to his use of the spur. Illogical though it may seem, those brightly shining, cheerily spinning and jingling ornaments which are attached, like the weathervane on a house, to the crown of a cowboy's hat have been participants in some of the unhappier times of Occident history, including the early Reproachful Years, the Lynching of the Insufferable Idea incident, and the Shumacher Shame and Truculence Decade.

Spurs were introduced in the Occident during the Windmill Remembrance Years after the hardy desert cattle breeds—the Spiny Angus, Bactrian Hereford, and Chihuahuan Shorthorn—replaced the traditional longhorn. Since the cattle no longer needed water, the windmills became obsolete. They fell into disrepair and were torn down and removed on some ranches, including the Merton and Shumacher ranches.

The cowboys soon became homesick for the familiar landmark, the tall, rickety structure with its friendly, companionably clanking, creaking, and rattling sail-wheel. Some of the cowboys gave voice to their yearning in the Sotol Saloon in Lindisfarne, where they were overheard by Betsy Hubschrauber II. Betsy was the founder and owner of the immensely profitable Pothole Park, which features a quarter-mile of highway bought by Betsy from the State of Oklahoma and moved intact to Lindisfarne, where it still draws thousands of amazed Texas visitors annually. Sensing a business opportunity, Betsy II put the research and development people in Hubschrauber's General Store to work on the Windmill Homesickness project. Within a few months they had developed the Windmill Hat, which was simply an ordinary cowboy hat such as the Flamboyant, the Heroic, or the Bullet-Riddled with a miniature windmill, including a fully operable sail-wheel and vane, installed over the crown.

"We liked them from the start," Miguel Cervantes, the foreman of the Kalplish Ranch, recalled many years later. "They were about a foot and a half high, with an eight-inch sail-wheel. The legs of the tower came right down over the crown and were bolted to the brim of the hat. The windmills were well-made; the sail-wheel turned in the gentlest breeze imaginable. They made a lot of difference for a bunch of lonely cowboys. Their racket was erratic, kind of, like conversation, and most of us felt they improved the quality of our lives.

"It was a pretty sight, I can tell you, to see the whole outfit all mounted up and fanning out across the range with those sail-wheels a-spinning, and the pump rods working up and down like they were pumping water right out of our hats, or our brains, which of course they weren't. They just went in through the crown of the hat and ended there, tapping us on the head sort of friendly like."

Cervantes concluded, "And that flapdoodle about the cowboy who took off into a strong headwind after a runaway cow and found himself and his horse sailing along four or five feet off the ground was just nonsense some Eastern newspaper made up. You had to watch out for tree limbs, though."

For the time the device was called a hat-windmill, but it was renamed because of Hurley Perkins' headaches. Perkins, the Kalplish Ranch wrangler, loved his hat windmill; the noise it made, however, gave him frequent headaches, so that he rode up to the chuckwagon daily to ask the cook, Juan Dirksen, who kept the aspirin, for "two more of them durn 'spurn, I reckon, for this here headache." The term was transferred from the cure of the headache to its cause, and eventually shortened

to *spur*. The sail-wheel came to be called a *rowel* because of the noise it made when it got rusty—"somewhere between a roar and a howl," Perkins once said. Yet another word was created to describe a spur which had got so rusty it would not turn and therefore refused to "talk" to its owner, or *spurned* him. Resourceful cowboys, recognizing the potential of the rowel, have often harnessed the energy of the little wheel. Miguel Cervantes, who suffered from poor circulation, hooked up a thumb-sized generator to his spur and used the current to heat his socks. Valentine Finch, the foreman of the Shumacher Ranch, installed a spotlight on his hat. Randall Sanchez, a cowboy on the same ranch, loved the sound of his spur so much that he connected the rowel to an amplifier.

Spurs have, oddly enough, been worn by cowboys on their heels during certain short, aberrant periods of Occident history. The first of these began on the Merton Ranch in the 1880's, when Oliver Merton hired sixteen-year-old Numero Herrenmeyer and several other serious, highly conscientious young men as green hands. They proved to be quick learners and showed promise of becoming first-rate cowboys. A few months after hiring them, however, Merton noticed one morning as the crew rode off toward Badger Flats that his younger cowboys had removed their spurs from their hats and attached them to their boots.

"Well, if that isn't the blamedest—" Merton exploded, and then stood open-mouthed, too stunned to continue.

"Ain't it?" Ralph Garza, Numero's uncle and a veteran Merton Ranch brandpainter, rode up beside Oliver. "I should've said something to you about it, but I kept thinking it was just some boyish prank of theirs and they'd get over it."

"How long has this been going on?" Merton asked.

Ralph scratched the generous bulge of his stomach reflectively. "Well, I guess I first noticed Numero doing it the day after he let those yearlings kill themselves when they stampeded over Lajitas Bluff."

"Why, that's been two months ago," Merton said.

"Yessir. Then there was those Spiny Angus cows we bought from the

Kalplish Ranch. Cesar Hamaker II put his spur on his heel after he brand-painted them on the wrong side."

Merton nodded. "I gave him what-for myself about that."

Ralph continued, "Then about a month ago a couple of those other young fellows let the mountain lions eat those colts. And they put *their* spurs on their heels right after that."

Merton began to scratch his stomach too. He said, "Well, there seems to be some kind of pattern to it, but damned if I can see what it is."

What it was, of course, was the beginning of the Reproachful Years, when the young cowboys, anxious to do their best for their employer, for the cows and horses, for the other members of the outfit, and for their own self-esteem, over-reacted to their slightest mistakes by attaching their spur to the heel of their boot and using it in its new, dangerous position to punish themselves.

"They replaced the sail-wheel, or rowel, with a sharp-pointed wheel," Miguel Cervantes recalled later. "They even had names for the vicious blamed things: cactus wheel, hex-dagger rowel, star blade. It was a sad time, I can tell you, and even sadder to come up over a hill above some lonely draw on the ranch and see a young cowboy down there walking alongside his horse and jabbing himself reproachfully with his spur in his rear or in his other leg."

Shocked by the movement, which spread to every ranch in the Occident, the ranchers quickly imposed rules on their crews to stop the spur-gellants: spurs were to be worn on the hat, and nowhere else; anyone caught with a spur on his boot would have to turn in his Authentic Cowboy certificate.

It wasn't enough, however.

"The very nature of our work made it almost impossible to catch these fine, but overly scrupulous, young fellows," Cervantes said, "because their duties took them to the most isolated places on earth, which is to say, the most isolated places in the Occident. Some of the cooks started issuing Mercurochrome along with the cowboys' rations of jerky and hoecake."

At the height of the Reproachful Years, hoping to deter the worst offenders, Oliver Merton proposed that a Calf Inspection be held during the monthly Marlboro Pose training sessions, which all the cowboys attended in Lindisfarne. Other ranchers agreed to the idea, but Valentine Finch, the leading defender of civil rights among the ranch outfits, quickly pointed out that such an inspection, even if meant for their own good, would violate the cowboys' rights. The move was dropped.

As often happens when it seems that a situation is hopeless, time cured the problem. As they grew older Numero Herrenmeyer and the other young cowboys became more skillful, and they let fewer cattle run over cliffs, drown in flash floods, or bloat on Johnson grass. And as they became better cowboys, they all moved their spurs from their heels back onto their hats.

Near the end of the Reproachful Years, however, the spurgellants' practice of wearing their spurs on the heels resulted, more or less directly, in the only lynching that ever occurred in the Texas Occident.

The incident began when Villalobos Smith, the bright young cattle rustler, and Numero Herrenmeyer got into a friendly argument in the Sotol Saloon about the merits of their horses. Villalobos' pinto, Avalanche, was, despite his notoriously coarse sense of humor, reputed to be the fastest horse in the Occident, and Villalobos was understandably proud of him. On the day in question Numero had ridden into town on Spirithoof, the incandescently beautiful Arabian mare who was destined to become the Merton Ranch flaghorse in later years. As the conversation became more heated and boastful, others in the saloon sensed that a race was in the offing, and word rapidly spread across town.

One of the first to hear about the race was the Mayor of Lindisfarne, Panther Junction Miranda, inventor of the Mayor Miranda Mitten and a man universally recognized as both an able public servant and a person unable to resist betting on a horse race. P.J., as he was called, ran to the saloon, and by the time Smith and Herrenmeyer had agreed to the race P.J. had already placed bets with two dozen people, putting all his money on Spirithoof, whose silvery beauty had blinded him to any question about whether she could actually run or not.

The formalities of the race were quickly settled. It was to be held on Lindisfarne's Main Street, and the distance was marked off from in front of Harnsgartner's Tanning Salon, the start, to the finish line between the Sotol Saloon and Hubschrauber's General Store across the street. The horses were to run a quarter of a mile.

The young riders removed the saddles from their horses to lighten their burden, mounted up, and rode to the starting line, Herrenmeyer wearing his spur on his boot while Smith's spur, of course, was on his hat. The street had filled with spectators eager to see the two well-known horses race, and the crowd left only a narrow lane for the competitors.

When the race began, it was immediately apparent that Spirithoof was outmatched in brute strength and speed, and in racing savvy. Avalanche bolted instantly to a length-and-a-half lead, and his supporters gave a great shout, for he seemed to be pulling farther ahead with every step. But they had not reckoned with the indomitable heart of Spirithoof, whose determination and courage had no equal in the Occident. Her nostrils flared, her eyes widened, she laid her ears flat and stretched out, more graceful and streamlined than a greyhound, and she began to gain on Avalanche.

The crowd's hullabaloo grew deafening as the horses passed the halfway point. Spirithoof had closed to within a length, and many could see, for the first time in his illustrious career, doubt in the eyes of Avalanche.

No one was more excited than Panther Junction Miranda, and when the beautiful Spirithoof continued to close on Avalanche, he threw reason to the wind. As the horses passed the three-quarter mark, he shouted at Numero Herrenmeyer, "Spur her! Just a little more and you'll win! Jab her with your rowel!"

The horses raced a few more lengths, perhaps not believing what they had heard. Miranda shouted again, "Spur her! You're going to win!" The horses slowed, their riders, who were as puzzled as their horses, straightened up, and then the horses stopped directly in front of Miranda.

"Spur her!" Miranda, who seemed oblivious of what was happening, shouted once more. "Jab her with the rowel!"

Avalanche, whose sense of humor was so gauche as to be legendary, suddenly laughed harshly in the silence, and that seemed to bring P.J. to his senses.

"Spur—" P.J. began yet again, and then he realized that the race had stopped, and the street was quieter than it had been since the first cornerstone was laid in Lindisfarne. His voice was the only sound to be heard. And the eye of every man, woman, child, and horse was fastened on him, aghast with disbelief and loathing.

"You understand, P.J., there's nothing vindictive at all in this," Tad Kalplish I said as he adjusted the noose around Miranda's neck a few minutes later. Since he had known Miranda the longest, Kalplish had been chosen to perform the unhappy formalities of the hanging. Their friendship dated as far back even as the pre-Civil War Barbed Wire Morality Discussions.

Kalplish continued, "We all like you as much as ever, and we'll miss you a whole lot. But while we all have a fierce belief in freedom of thought and speech, there is, finally, a limit. You have given voice to an Insufferable Idea, and being as how we can't hang an idea, we have to hang the next best thing, which is you."

"I don't begrudge it atall, Tad," P.J. answered, "and I'm right proud that you're knotting up this handsome rope for me." He nodded appreciatively at Tad I's personal lariat, which had been woven in a plaid Campbell Watch pattern and had a cashmere fringe. "I'm happy to die, for I'd rather be dead anytime than have to remember the hurt in Spirithoof's eyes when she looked at me."

So the lynching of the Insufferable Idea took place, and there are, to this day, no citizens of the Occident who willingly discuss it—and also, of course, none who have ever broached Panther Junction Miranda's idea again.

Ironically, the Shumacher Shame and Truculence Decade also involved cowboys' wearing spurs on the heels of their boots—not one boot, as had been the case in the Reproachful Years, but both.

Historians believe the problem first surfaced in the spring of 1930 or 1931, in early April. For a few weeks during that time, old-timers recall, cowboys from the Shumacher Ranch were impossible to get along with. They quarreled at the slightest provocation with cowboys from other outfits, and they even fought among themselves.

"They'd all started wearing their spurs on their boots," Miguel Cervantes remembers, "not just one, but both boots. None of us had ever seen anything like it. They changed the sail-wheel—the rowel. It didn't look like a windmill wheel any more. And every time some cowboy from another ranch'd say something about it, no matter how friendly he said it, he'd find himself in a fight."

Cervantes added, "Of course I suspected—I reckon a lot of others did too—that Marie Shumacher had something to do with the trouble, since she was always into one kind of orneriness or another. But everyone held her in such reverence that you just didn't give voice to that kind of suspicion."

By early May, however, although they would not discuss the cause of their bad tempers, the Shumacher cowboys seemed to have returned to normal, and most of them put their spurs back on their hats. Then, for a few weeks in September, they became truculent again. After that they settled down and there were no more troubles until the following April, when the cowboys flared up once more.

"It was nerve-wracking," Cervantes wrote later. "For a while when we met them we didn't know whether to say howdy or run. But gradually we began to understand when their highs and lows were—that's what we called their temper shifts, seasonal highs and lows—and to know when to avoid them. But it was damned inconvenient. And what they were doing to their spurs, particularly the rowels, was downright obscene."

What they were doing was radically changing the rowel; it no longer resembled a windmill's sail-wheel at all, with separate sails to catch the wind, but was made of a single piece of metal cast or forged into a slightly concave shape, much like a dinner plate, and about the same size. Its edges were sharpened, resulting in spurs that could be dangerous weapons. They were, in fact, put to use on more than one occasion during the Shame and Truculence Decade by the Shumacher cowboys during their lows. Some of them became adept at suddenly turning a half-cartwheel and standing on their hands, so that a cowboy from another ranch who had thought he was getting into a fistfight found himself facing two large, knife-sharp, disk-like weapons.

The weapons were, quite literally, disks, and Miguel Cervantes' unvoiced suspicion that Marie Shumacher was involved in the bizarre behavior of the Shumacher cowboys proved well-founded. Marie Shumacher was that same Marie Macleoud who was captured by a band of Comanches at the age of ten and, six years later, a wildly beautiful young woman, rescued by Arturo Shumacher II in one of the most dramatic and daring deeds ever performed in the Texas Occident. Although her unpredictable, willful, and sometimes overtly sensational conduct had often shocked and angered the Occident, the revered matriarch of the Shumacher Ranch was so much part and parcel of its tradition and history that, ultimately, she could do no wrong.

Ironically, Pickup IV, the great-grandaughter of the cow which fell from the top of Ordnance Butte, smashed in the rear of Marie Shumacher's 1909 French Panhard sedan, and caused Mrs. Shumacher to become deranged for some time, was the cow responsible for the revelation of the Shumacher Shame. Pickup IV, who was and still is generally regarded in the Occident as the most mischievous and downright malevolent cow ever to annihilate a five-wire fence, had escaped as usual during the spring roundup on the Merton Ranch. Armando Miller and two other cowboys had chased her across fifteen miles of barren desert, eventually reaching the Shumacher Ranch fence line not far from the Cabora Creek crossing. Pickup IV, again as usual, crashed through the fence and continued galloping tirelessly toward the East Cabora Creek lowlands.

"Pickup IV topped the rise over the lowlands," Armando recalled, "and then she just sat down on her rear, put her forefeet out, and skidded to a stop. I've never seen a more astonished cow."

The cowboys rode up beside her, and they too stopped, astounded. In the valley below they saw all the cowhands of the Shumacher Ranch, half of them on their horses and the other half lined up on foot along one side of the few acres of flatland on the floor of the little valley. Each man on foot was holding onto the end of a lariat which was tied to the saddlehorn of the horse in front of him.

"Everyone of them that was on foot was swearing a blue streak," Armando reported. "I never heard such bad language in all my days."

At the end of the little valley Marie Shumacher herself sat in a rocking chair on the flattened rear end of her French Panhard, which she still drove. She raised her hand, and the cowboys quieted down, although they were still grumbling.

"Ready?" Marie shouted. She dropped her hand. "PLOW!"

"The horses leaned forward and started walking," Armando recalled. "The cowboys on foot leaned backwards against their ropes, swearing worse than ever. They dug their spurs into the ground, and the horses started pulling them across the flat. And then we all realized at the same time, Pickup IV and the rest of us, what Marie was making them do: they were tandem-disking that five-acre field. Well, Pickup IV just fell over on the ground laughing, and then so did we, and our horses too."

What Marie Shumacher was suffering from, of course, was an advanced form of *seniculture*, that ailment of old age that makes one desire to turn a ranch into a farm. Much to the relief of the Shumacher cowboys, she recovered two years later, lost interest in farming, and began to raise hamsters and chinchillas. And the cowhands put their spurs back on their hats. But to this day cowboys from other outfits remember that April used to be ground-breaking time on the Shumacher Ranch and September was when everything was plowed under, and they step very lightly around the Shumacher crew during those months.

SIX-GUN IV
The Lonely Duel

T he winter snow blanketed the desert, and melted; spring came to the Texas Occident, the bluebonnets bloomed, and at last even the cautious mesquites leafed out. And in Lindisfarne, in the dusty street between the Sotol Saloon and Hubschrauber's General Store, nine months after their gun battle had begun, Randall Sanchez and Cesar Hamaker still faced each other, their jaws set, their intense eyes never wavering.

In May, after more than half a year of silence, Valentine Finch received a letter from Augustus Kalplish, the private detective. He was under a doctor's care in Beaumont, Texas. The trail of the pants thief Cal Clinnjin had led him on a tortuous chase from Little Rock through the Ozarks and then into the Big Thicket, where for months he had looked behind every tree and under every bush, feeling Clinnjin's presence so intensely sometimes, he reported, that "I knew what kind of tooth powder he was using." One afternoon in mid-April, Kalplish leaped snarling into a large hollow tree, sure that he had finally cornered his man. Unfortunately the tree contained only a black bear, also snarling, and so Kalplish lost many months while he recuperated. He had, however, hired an assistant who was confidently tracking Clinnjin and Cesar Hamaker's keys in the general direction of Denver.

While Augustus Kalplish recovered in Beaumont from his encounter with a bear and his assistant tracked the pants thief who had the keys to Cesar Hamaker's toxboxes, and while Leticia Harnsgartner's mother languished in debt in Jamaica, her search for Randall Sanchez's keys stymied for the time being, life went on in Lindisfarne, despite the drama being played out in the street between the Sotol Saloon and Hubschrauber's General Store.

In August of 1874, a full year after the Sanchez-Hamaker gunfight started, the two ranchers whose cowboys were involved in the dispute, Arturo Shumacher I and Oliver Merton, were overheard complaining bitterly in The Bean Sprout, a popular restaurant.

"This damned humanitarian count-to-ten-and-then-some nonsense your crew started has cost us two good hands for God knows how long," Oliver groused.

"Well, one good hand anyway," Arturo said. "If they'd just shoot and be done with it, one would most likely be dead."

"One beats none," Oliver replied.

The conversation resulted in a much-praised innovation. Merton and Shumacher, at their own expense, established the well-known "withdraw to draw" toxbox keyboxes in the vault at the Lindisfarne Bank. There the ranchers and cowboys might keep their keys on a twenty-four-hour notice arrangement, thus enabling them to shoot each other within, as Merton and Shumacher asserted in a joint announcement printed in the Weekly Gatherer, "a more reasonable period of time, when angry passions are still at a high pitch and need not be re-stimulated in order for the killer and killee to experience a satisfying catharsis."

The searches for the missing keys stretched into a year, and then more years. Leticia Harnsgartner's mother's house and whatnot collection were auctioned off in Hartford, Connecticut, and she resumed her chase, but by spring 1875, when she finally discovered in Panama that her son Amos had taken ship for Mombasa, on the east cost of Africa, she had exhausted her funds again. Demoralized, barely conscious, and now afflicted with malaria, she was about to despair and have herself and her hospital bed, which was in a state of collapse, sent back to Hartford, where she no longer had a home, when a large cash contribution arrived for her from an anonymous donor. Wasting no time in speculating who her—and Randall Sanchez's—benefactor was, she set sail for Mombasa.

In the late 1870's Cesar Hamaker began to complain of arthritic pains in his shoulders and knees. With Randall's generous approval, citizens of Lindisfarne occasionally stopped to massage his aches, or, on cold mornings, to bring him hotpads. Randall's left boot disintegrated, but he was mysteriously fitted with new boots made of numerous exotic skins. The counter, vamps, and wingtips of the boots were elaborately carved, and the tops were virtual works of art.

"I don't know," Randall answered when a reporter from the *Weekly Gatherer* asked him who had given him the boots. "Someone just picked me up in the dark and put 'em on me."

It was never determined who began the practice of decorating the two gunfighters for Christmas. The popular story was that on Christmas Eve in 1880 or '81 Genevieve Krebs, a destitute but good-hearted little orphan girl, was running home to her hovel with a package of foil icicles for her scrawny tree when she noticed the crouching figures of Randall and Cesar, drab and lonely in the fading light. Although the icicles would have been her tree's only decoration, she was overcome with pity for the two men, and she draped the entire contents of the package over them.

Others, more cynical, suggested that the Lindisfarne Chamber of Commerce had clandestinely decorated the men in an attempt to keep them in the media spotlight. At any rate, decorating the gunfighters grew to be such a popular ritual that it eventually began on Thanksgiving Day and became so elaborate that both men complained, "We can't hardly stand up, we got so much durn stuff put on us." When electric lights were introduced, Randall was shocked repeatedly one wet night until Betsy Hubschrauber, now the many-bowed owner of a justly famous emporium which sprawled over an entire city block, heard his groans and ran out to unplug the shorting string of bulbs.

Augustus Kalplish, recovered at last from the mauling given him by the bear in the Big Thicket, encountered a baffling situation in Sacramento in 1890. He finally ran the diabolically elusive Cal Clinnjin to ground, only to discover that the pants thief had died peacefully in his own bed in 1887. Clinnjin's will had been probated, and various unopened boxes had been distributed among his eight children. One of these boxes, Kalplish was sure, contained the keys to Cesar Hamaker's toxboxes, but the children were scattered all over the country. Resigned to his fate, Augustus began hunting for them, starting with the eldest, Oren Clinnjin, who, the detective discovered in 1894, was a potato farmer near Pocatello, Idaho.

In the meantime, Leticia Harnsgartner's mother's search for the keys to Randall Sanchez's toxboxes had become more extensive with each passing year. Money in ever-increasing amounts came from her unknown benefactor, and she used it to hire agents whom she sent in every direction around the world as rumors of sightings of her son reached her. In 1901 she decided that the time she spent managing her army of agents no longer allowed her to conduct a personal search. She returned to Hartford, Connecticut, where she was already a legend, for she had been reported dead at least a dozen times. In Hartford she bought a mansion and set up a command headquarters. Finding herself a celebrity in her hometown, she literally sprang from her hospital bed, took dancing lessons, and began to live nearly as extravagantly as her prodigal son.

It was in November of that same year that citizens of Lindisfarne first heard what became known as the Hamaker Howl. "It is a rudimentary howl," the *Weekly Gatherer* reported, "that would bristle the hackles of the dullest man alive and send the savagest pit bull whining under the house." Lindisfarners, intimately familiar with the voices of both gunfighters, knew immediately that it was Cesar Hamaker, not Randall Sanchez, who was howling. The ghastly sounds occurred around midnight about twice a week that first winter, causing adults to sit bolt upright in bed and children to run weeping to their parents' arms. The next winter, 1902, the howls increased in frequency "and," the *Weekly Gatherer* said, "in intensity, if that is possible." By 1904 they lasted from early fall to late spring and were shattering the night four times a week. It was clear that something had to be done.

"Even on the nights he doesn't howl, no one sleeps," the *Gatherer* reported, "for no one can bear the thought of being ripped out of peaceful somnolence by the jagged jaws of that terrible howl."

Psychologists were called in. They identified the sound as "a howl of primal loneliness," and, with many witnesses present, they questioned Cesar Hamaker, and Randall Sanchez too, but learned nothing.

"Are you unhappy?" Cesar was asked by a psychologist from the University of Texas at Austin.

"I reckon no more than any other man who's run into a little delay," he answered.

"Nothing extraordinary is bothering you?"

"My arthritis sometimes, but folks have been real good about that."

"So, other than the fact that you've had to stand here in the street for a prolonged length of time, you don't feel inconvenienced?"

Cesar thought for a moment. "Well, the dogs are kind of a nuisance."

"And the pigeons," Randall added.

The psychologist said, "Do you feel lonely? After all, you have Randall here for company."

"Yes sir, and he's generally good company, even if I am going to shoot his damned head off."

"So if you're not lonely, why do you howl at night?"

Cesar studied the toes of his boots and mumbled sullenly, "I don't know."

The psychologist turned to Randall. "Why do you think Cesar howls?"

Randall too looked down. He replied shamefacedly, "I don't know."

So the mystery was not solved. Oddly, it was Leticia Harnsgartner, not Betsy Hubschrauber, who saw the opportunity to profit from the Hamaker Howl. She put in a stock of ear plugs at Old West Aerobics, which she had opened next to her tanning salon in response to the demand from many cowboys for help in developing their bowlegs. Despite the still-heavy volume of trade in Betsy's huge store, it was whispered that her capital had been severely depleted, perhaps through ill-advised foreign investments.

(Continued: See SIX-GUN V)

BRANDPAINTING

Eighty-five members of the American Animal Fairness League arrived in the Texas Occident in the summer of 1948. They stepped off the train in Lindisfarne warily, certain of an unfriendly reception, perhaps even violence.

"They came," the editor of the Lindisfarne *Weekly Gatherer* wrote, "accompanied by federal marshals and armed with injunctions to stop the 'inhuman and arbitrary, nefariously cruel and unnatural practice of brandpainting.' They had heard so much—as who has not?—about the fanatic upholding of tradition in the Texas Occident that many expected armed resistance, and some had predicted that the train would be ambushed before it arrived. Thus, their actual welcome in Lindisfarne was a pleasant surprise."

Stunning would have been a better adjective. Burly ranchers ran to the AAFL team members, flung their arms around their necks, and wept copiously. Bearded cowboys, their faces weathered by all of heat and cold and wind that Nature could hurl at them, kissed embarrassed federal marshals on either cheek.

The *Gatherer* reported, "The ranchers and cowboys welcomed the AAFL representatives with a relief that in its pathetic sincerity would have wrenched the granite heart of a statue—but there was also fearfulness. To be told—nay, ordered!—to stop what every cowboy had yearned to stop doing for many decades—that is, brandpainting the ever more complex and idiosyncratic designs demanded by the cows of the Texas

Occident—would seem to be a heaven-sent command indeed. To be told to stop what had started nearly a hundred years earlier, however innocently, as a cowboy's attempt to placate a few envious cows, an attempt which had burgeoned into what the rancher Tad Kalplish II once called 'the godawfulest damned can of worms ever exploded in Texas,' was every cowboy's dream. Such an order would seem to be cause for great rejoicing. And to some extent it was; but to every thoughtful and knowledgeable human in the Texas Occident, it was also cause for the utmost trepidation. 'I fear, I fear!' was the prophetic wail of Marie Shumacher, the revered matriarch of the Shumacher Ranch."

And well she should have. The AAFL teams arrived a few days before brandpainting season was to start, when cows were queued up by age and rank for many miles on every ranch. Word of what these strangers fanning out across the countryside intended to do passed like wildfire among the herds, and the reaction of the cows was quick and drastic. Within three weeks of the arrival of the AAFL teams, despite their frantic attempts at forced-feeding when they discovered too late that the cattle had gone on a hunger strike, more than 400 head had starved to death. Additionally, according to Big Springs Madison, a veterinarian writing in the *Journal of Occidental Bovinity*, "Nearly 20,000 have suffered such trauma that the probability of their ever again being able to function fully in the social structure of the Texas Occident is highly doubtful."

In the scandal and outcry that followed, the AAFL teams quickly packed and sneaked out of the Occident, and the problem of brandpainting was once again squarely on the shoulders of the ranchers and cowboys.

The story of how the laborious and economically disastrous practice of brandpainting began has been told and retold around campfires in the Texas Occident for over a century now, and the bitterness and sorrow of storyteller and listeners alike have become rooted more deeply in each generation.

The tale begins with the arrival on the Kalplish Ranch of a footsore band of Comanche warriors, fewer than a dozen in number, armed with

a hammerless musket and a few bows and arrows and leading two bony
yearling colts. The dispirited warriors, after suffering a sound defeat in
an attack on the village of Mala Vista on the Rio Grande, had retreated
to Cabora Creek and followed it upstream until they came to a spring on
the Kalplish Ranch. There they camped for several weeks, after first assur-
ing the ranch foreman, Miguel Cervantes, of their peaceful intentions.

"I had never seen more demoralized human beings," Cervantes wrote
to a friend later; "their belligerence was less than a ground squirrel's.
Their decorative feathers drooped, and the strings on their bows were
rotten. I saw no manifestation of the warlike ferocity we commonly
associated with the Comanches."

Except, Cervantes should have added, in their preoccupation with
their half-starved colts, a pair of mustangs of muddy-dun color. Every
day, using the bright clays from the bottom of Cabora Creek, the warriors painted the colts with the ancient war symbols of the plains: the
jagged bolt of lightning, the puma's hooked claws, the teeth of wolves
and beaks of eagles, the thorny circle of eternity and death.

And every day the lean, bristly-haired cows which Tad Kalplish I had
segregated in a pasture at the spring, the same hardy mutants which
had shown special adaptative characteristics for the desert and which
would be among the ancestors of the Bactrian Hereford, Chihuahuan
Shorthorn, and Spiny Angus breeds to be introduced a few generations
later, gathered at the creek. They came not for water, for they drank
no more than a lizard; they came to watch the Comanches painting
the mustang colts.

Cervantes wrote, "We knew already that the desert cattle breeds, the
ones with the best water-retention abilities, were a swaggering, conceited
lot, vain and jealous to the point of stupidity, more apt to pause and
admire their reflection in a mud puddle, should they ever find one in
the desert, than to drink from it; but what we had not reckoned with
was their stubbornness. Every day the cows watched the warriors painting the colts, and every day they retreated more reluctantly from the
creek to graze; they began to follow me, and the other cowboys, especially

the wrangler, Hurley Perkins, with their eyes, their large, mutely pleading eyes, until we dreamt of them at night, until first one of us and then another awoke in the bunkhouse, those great round eyes with that inexorable, indelible plea burnt into our brains. And when we stepped out of the bunkhouse in the morning, it was to face a silent semicircle of those same eyes, watching, waiting; waiting. But they hounded Hurley Perkins the most, for they seemed to sense that he was the weakest link."

Finally Perkins could take no more. "The cook, Juan Dirksen, was whitewashing the chuckwagon," Cervantes wrote. "At about mid-morning on June 5, 1858, Hurley walked up to the chuckwagon, snatched the paintbrush from his hand, and grabbed the can of paint. 'Where are you going with that paint, Hurley?' Juan asked. Hurley replied, 'I'm going to stop those damned cows from pestering me, once and for all.' Little did he know that, rather than stopping something, he was starting it."

The cows, about two dozen of them, were gathered as usual to watch the painting of the colts. They saw Hurley coming and quickly fathomed his intentions. "They seemed to have planned it all in advance," Cervantes wrote. "They fell into a rough line, and each presented her left flank. And if cattle can smile, they were smiling. Coming to Persephone, the oldest of the cows, who was first in line, Hurley hesitated, thinking what he should paint. Would God he had turned and run in that fateful moment! Instead, he stepped forward and painted, in short, brisk strokes, a simple capital letter K on Persephone's left flank. And the die was cast."

Perkins' choice of the letter K was the cause of one of the numerous misconceptions about brandpainting in later years, for many outsiders assumed it was meant to indicate ownership of the cattle by Tad Kalplish I. "Nothing could be further from the truth, of course, for our cattle were as free to come and go as we were, and we detested the notion that one creature might own another," Cervantes wrote. "Hurley had simply hoped to instill some literacy among the cows by using a letter of the alphabet, and he also wanted to avoid the warlike signs the warriors were painting on the colts. So he thought, 'K for Comanche,' and painted it. His spelling wasn't so good in those days."

It was a puzzling experience for Hurley. No sooner had he painted a K on a cow's flank than she galloped off, bellowing with happiness. And every one galloped off in a different direction. At first Hurley was glad, for he thought it meant the cows had left the spring and gone off to graze. What each cow did in actuality, of course, was to gallop off in search of other cows in order to prance, preen, and strut about, glancing back over her left shoulder frequently to gloat at the freshly painted K on her flank. And the reaction of the other cows was predictable.

Hurley brandpainted all of the cows without stopping to rest, using the paint thriftily yet carefully filling in the serifs of each K. As he worked he heard a rumbling, as of thunder; the smell of dust stirring came to him, and he heard the bawling of cattle in the distance, but he paid little attention, wishing to finish the chore he had set for himself. Finally he painted the last K on the last cow, giving it a slightly italic slant, and he looked up with a sigh of relief that broke off abruptly: the Comanches had long since fled, taking their colts with them. Hurley was surrounded by 5,000 cows, all waiting to be brandpainted, and three times that many more were thundering across the desert toward the spring on Cabora Creek.

The curse of brandpainting has, since that day of mistaken kindliness, plagued the ranches of the Texas Occident. Somewhere between the ages of eleven and fourteen months, calves begin hanging around the ranchhouses, frightening wives and blocking the ranch roads. Their glazed, pleading eyes express their naked desire to be brandpainted, to pass through that ritual of puberty and receive the status symbol and proof of maturity. So pervasive and absolute is the symbol's importance that, as disgusted ranchers and cowboys have often attested, no matter how winsome a young heifer may be, herd sires will ignore her unless she is brandpainted.

Perhaps the most desperate effort to stop brandpainting was made on the Merton Ranch in 1912 when Oliver Merton, hoping that pain and fear would squelch vanity and conceit, ordered his cowboys to brandpaint with red-hot irons. The cowboys, as eager as Merton to stop the

odious practice, agreed to try his idea. But when the actual branding began and the bawling of tormented cows came to their ears, the smell of singed hair and burnt skin to their nostrils, cowboy after weeping cowboy threw down the hot iron and quit in disgust, appalled at the cruelty in which they were participating. Merton, although severely nauseated, continued to wield the iron himself until one of the remaining cowboys, Rudolfo Miller, tapped him on the shoulder. Merton looked up to see yearling heifers lining up for miles, and older cows, even those already brandpainted, leaping fences to join the queue, eager to have their skin seared and scarred in the name of fashion.

Accidents have also led the finicky, fad-enslaved cattle in new directions. One generation of cows insisted on having their ears split because Pickup IV, a cow on the Merton Ranch, slashed her ear on barbed wire while admiring a stretch of fence near Ordnance Butte that had been conceived and installed by the master barbed-wire artist, Lorenzo Dirksen, son of the pioneer Kalplish Ranch cook, Juan Dirksen. Other cows saw her savagely bifurcated ear, mistakenly assumed it had been cut by the Merton Ranch brandpainting crew, and queued up at the ranchhouse and refused to eat or drink until all their ears had been similarly mutilated by weeping cowboys who retched and even fainted in their horror of the ghastly work. Armando Miller, Rudolfo's son, accidentally daubed red paint on a cow's nose as he was turning to the paint barrel, and since then the cows have insisted on red-tinted noses. A similar misstep in 1895 by Arvil Judson, a line-rider on the Kalplish Ranch, resulted in dark lines being drawn around the eyes of every cow. An unnoticed hog ring in the ear of a heifer bought by Tad Kalplish II in San Antonio caused the Hog-Ring Stampede of 1926, and a ring discovered too late in the nose of a bull imported from Argentina resulted in the destruction of the famous twelve-sided Merton Ranch Corral in 1937. The word *stampede* itself, sometimes erroneously taken to derive from the Spanish word *estampida*, was first used on the Shumacher Ranch in 1870 to describe the rush of cattle to be branded, or stamped.

Although not all the innovations brought about accidentally or otherwise have resulted in a tragedy such as, in 1931, Del Rio Judson and Arturo Shumacher II became enmeshed in, their story epitomizes the despair and frustration felt in the Occident. Del Rio, a young cowboy and the son, ironically, of Arvil Judson, was sent to spend four months alone in a remote line camp on the Shumacher Ranch. Through faulty record-keeping, or perhaps simply forgetfulness, he was left there for six months. When Arturo Shumacher II remembered Del Rio, he was so conscience-stricken that he himself rode out to get him. About twenty miles from the line camp, however, to his surprise he met Del Rio walking in the direction of the ranch headquarters. The cowboy was leading a cow by means of a halter fashioned from leather whangs.

"Where's your horse, Del Rio?" Arturo asked.

"A mountain lion ate him last winter," Del Rio answered; "but it's all right. Me and this cow got to be friends, and I've become a sculptor. Look what I've done." He pointed to a large, incongruously shaped hump rising from between the cow's shoulder blades. It appeared to be made of dried, crushed grass mixed with mud and perhaps manure. "Ain't it pretty?"

As Arturo was about to answer, he heard a wistful lowing that seemed to come from many mouths in the distance behind Del Rio. Looking beyond the young cowboy, he saw, stretching for seven or eight miles, an unbroken line of cows, all wanting a sculpted hump on their backs. Drawing his gun, he shot Del Rio. Then he shot the cow too, and hurriedly scraped a hole in the rocky desert soil in which to bury her, cursing himself for not enlisting Del Rio's help to dig first before he shot him. But Shumacher's justifiable homicide—as the court later ruled in the case of both the cowboy and the cow—was too late. Del Rio, in his lonely creativity, had originated the spurious Brahma cattle breed, which still struts the range today showing off its artificial hump.

After using up the letters of the English alphabet and the Greek as well, the early brandpainters painted signs from the zodiac on the cattle, and after that various Pythagorean symbols. That was before the realization of the true nature of the desert cow's vanity, its extent and terrible pervasiveness, began to dawn upon them, and they understood that every variation, every change, no matter how simple, was in fact a complication, for the cows, insatiably vain and incomparably tasteless, always wanted more. Thus, when Numero Herrenmeyer, a young cowboy on the Shumacher Ranch, painted a brightly petaled daisy on a cow's flank in 1883, the cow studied it and smiled, but did not move on.

"What's with her?" Numero asked Alfonso Vela.

Alfonso snarled, "What's with her, stupid, is that she likes the daisy, but she wants all the rest painted on too—everything she had last year: the upsilon and omega, the Gemini sign, and the diagram and formulas for the Pythagorean Proposition. What's with the rest of the herd now is they all want the daisy too. And the next time you feel artsy, let me know first and we'll run you through the hay baler."

So the abyss between the artist and the practical needs of Occidental ranch life has also been a source of tension related to brandpainting, and still another has been the unwavering preference of the cattle for kitsch, for the very worst in contemporary taste. When Oliver Merton returned from Europe in 1900 full of enthusiasm for the bold primary colors of the Impressionists, many cowboys welcomed his ideas, thinking that an infusion of real art would break the tedium of brandpainting. To their disgust, the cows opted instead for a soggy, over-sentimentalized version of Romanticism. Similarly, the cows rejected the fresh, rational plane geometry of Mondrian on the one hand and the harshly perceptive irrationality of Kandinski on the other, their inclinations seldom rising above the level of illustrations for cereal boxes or lingerie advertisements.

"We're enslaved by the ignorant to do that to them which makes them look even more ignorant," Tad Kalplish III said in 1986; "and the more ignorant they look, the more they want to look ignorant. I wish we had more rain out here; then we could raise catfish and forget we ever saw a cow."

So far there's no rain in sight.

PICKUP

The controversy over the pickup has raged since its first appearance, and resolution seems as unlikely today as it was fifty years ago. Only the story of the quaint, ungainly conveyance's origin seems beyond dispute: that is, that following a ludicrous accident, a well-known rancher's wife, motivated either by hysteria or impulsive whimsy, caused the pickup to be introduced to the Texas Occident.

Like the Great Chicago Fire forty years earlier, the pickup disaster was also caused by a cow, an irascible brindle cow with a single stub horn, owned by the Merton ranch. She was known as Pickup because a cowboy, Mando Dirksen, formerly of the Kalplish Ranch, when told to drive the cow back into a corral after she had broken out, had replied, "Drive her? Gawddang it all, nobody can drive her. I druther pick up that old rip and carry her on my head than try to drive her."

During the ranch's fall roundup of 1911, Pickup broke away from the herd and led the same Mando Dirksen and another cowboy, Alfonso Vela, on a wild chase down Colpitts Canyon and up the west slope of Ordnance Butte. When they reached the flat top of the butte the two men, thinking they finally had her cornered, shook out their lariats, whooped, and spurred their horses after the cow. To their astonishment, instead of turning back when she reached the far edge, Pickup galloped on without slackening speed and leaped. The men pulled up their winded horses in time to see her bounce off a ledge thirty yards below, cartwheel through the air, hit a slope fifty yards farther down and roll,

bellowing, for another fifty before she again became airborne for fully
seventy yards, crashed through a thicket of junipers over the Terlingua
road, and smashed in the roof and landed upside-down in the back seat
of a 1909 French Panhard sedan driven by Marie Macleoud Shumacher,
wife of Arturo II. Pickup struggled to her feet, leaped out, and ran on
while Mrs. Shumacher screamed and the car swerved wildly.

When Mrs. Shumacher finally managed to stop the car, she too leaped
out and also ran down the road, shrieking, in the same direction, oddly
enough, that Pickup had taken. The cowboys watching from Ordnance
Butte, however, shouted at her repeatedly that there was no danger, and
at last she halted.

"Old Pickup fell on your car," Mando yelled; "that durned old brindle cow of Merton's."

"What?"

"Pickup," Alfonso shouted; "she fell on your car."

While she walked cautiously back to the Panhard, the cowboys advised
her, if the car would still run, to turn around and go home.

As she neared the car and observed its myopic, insect-like
appearance—the remaining passenger area rising from the flat body like
a surprised, bug-eyed question mark—Mrs. Shumacher began to chuckle,
then laugh outright. She got into the maimed vehicle, started it, and,
to the cowboy's surprise, the car lurched on toward Lindisfarne, its rear
wheels wobbling dangerously.

When she reached the town, she drove the length of Main Street
again and again, squeezing the bulb horn on the Panhard continuously.
Finally one of the wobbling rear wheels fell off, and the car stopped.
The astonished citizenry swarmed around asking what had happened,
but Mrs. Shumacher could only giggle uncontrollably and stammer
"Pickup, Pickup."

Thereafter, every Sunday afternoon and often on weekdays, Mrs.
Shumacher haunted the streets of Lindisfarne in her strangely malformed
automobile, replying to all queries, "Pickup, Pickup." Young Monahans
Macleoud, son of the pioneer Lindisfarne bootmaker, himself a half-

brother to Mrs. Shumacher, and the newly hired editor of the *Weekly Gatherer*, apparently was the first to warn of the danger posed, however inadvertently, for the community. Noting that "already susceptible young ladies, and even young men, are gazing yearningly at this repulsive means of transport," Macleoud urged in the March 8, 1912 issue of the *Gatherer* that "the wife of a prominent area citizen, justifiably prominent in her own right, who, because of our boundless regard and reverence for her, shall remain nameless in these columns except in paragraphs of praise, refrain from debasing our streets, and worse, from turning the heads of our easily-swayed young people, with this ugly, useless, wheeled abomination which they have begun to covet, and which they call Pickup," and failing that, that "our township fathers take action instanter to ban this vileness from our streets and our sight now, and forever."

Even as the newspaper was being printed that Wednesday, however, Coyanosa Merton, the eldest daughter of the rancher whose cow had started the trouble, stopped the family Oldsmobile under Leaning Tree Rock, twelve miles west of Lindisfarne, and persuaded three young men who were never positively identified to push the rock over on the rear portion of the car. Later the same day Raul Vinson, apparently acting in concert with the Merton girl, backed his father's Winton under the cattle-loading chute at the railway yards. That afternoon, while bystanders gawked, Mrs. Shumacher's Panhard was joined by two more half-wrecked vehicles parading Main Street, their drivers mindlessly shouting "Pickup! Pickup!"

"Too late, too late!" Macleoud lamented in the next issue of the *Gatherer*, and he asked, more prophetically than he knew, "What plague have we loosed upon ourselves?"

What was loosed in the decades following the flattening of Mrs. Shumacher's Panhard was intense competition among American auto makers in a determined and sometimes vicious effort to corner the trend-setting pickup market of the Texas Occident. Through it all, despite the ballyhoo of the manufacturers and the mad dashes every year for this model or that by gullible buyers, the basic configuration of the pickup—an upright "cab" area, like a windowed outhouse, ahead of a flat, useless "bed"—has remained unchanged. The first models sold in Lindisfarne apparently were produced in the same general way as the Merton's daughter, Coyanosa, and Raul Vinson had made theirs. A Ford dealer, however, advertised in the 1913 *Gatherer* "Twenty-five Pickup sedans, cow-flattened in the great Texas Occident tradition." The vehicles were snapped up in three days, despite an outraged Chevrolet dealer's claim that he personally had seen the cars being smashed in by a gang with sledge hammers on a railway siding west of San Antonio.

Various manufacturers made cow-drop claims during the next two years, but the scarcity of materials and labor during the first World War eventually forced Detroit to abandon all pretense concerning the expensive extra steps involved in first fabricating, then destroying the rear sedan area. By 1919 every pickup bed was made in the same simple, functionless shape. The *Gatherer*, which had from the beginning resisted the pickup influx vigorously, and always unsuccessfully, was prompted to snarl in a 1920 editorial, "Not only can we not rid ourselves of these loutish self-propelled carts; now they are pushed upon us in scabrous imitation of their traditional manufacture, which, ludicrous as it was, had nonetheless set a tradition."

Little change was made in the pickup during the Depression years and World War II. Whether motivated by tradition or perverseness, the basic expectations of the pickup owner that his vehicle be battered and awkward-looking, as well as impractical, were satisfied by the circumstances of the times. The same inertia was true of the early fifties, although Studebaker, in a last-gasp attempt to regain a share of the market, introduced a model which, ironically, would prove to be the most profound influence on pickup design in the late seventies; yet it was met by vehement opposition at the time.

Studebaker gambled its future on the results of a survey by the *Gatherer* of 8,000 pickup beds in the spring of 1954. "We found," the *Gatherer* reported, "fifty-three pickup beds which had nothing at all in them except road dust; twenty-four containing spare tires, nineteen of which were flat; three containing saddles; three with a partial bale of decomposing alfalfa hay; one fully loaded with prairie hay, although this pickup had apparently been abandoned some months or years earlier, for its wheels and engine were missing; and 7,916 pickup beds with from one to two hundred and seventy-nine empty beer cans in them, and nothing else."

Characteristically years ahead of its time, Studebaker drastically altered its assembly line and revamped its fall advertising campaign to introduce the PC (pre-canned) pickup, which featured an empty Falstaff can welded in the left front corner of the bed. It was easily the most talked-about event of the 1954 season, and Studebaker's competitors, caught off-guard, held their breath while the Occident made up its mind. Unfortunately for Studebaker, the verdict was negative.

"It's a great idea," the *Gatherer* quoted one buyer of a new Dodge as he signed a promissory note at the Lindisfarne Cattleman's Bank; "but you have to come on slow here. The fact is, we're just not ready for the PC."

New technology in the early sixties brought with it what Jesus Perkins, president of the Pickup Owners of Occidental Texas Association, has called "the most painful moral dilemma in pickup history." The *Gatherer*, sworn enemy of the pickup for over half a century, crowed in a 1963 editorial, "Lo the woeful pickup driver, that grimy, rough-edged paragon of Wild West toughness: how he swelters in his air-conditioned cab! how he braves the elements, immersed in stereophonic music! how recklessly he slumps on his contoured seat, his pillowed armrest! how the carpeted floor torments his feet! what dexterity and strength his automatic shift, power steering, and power brakes require! how he squints into the merciless sun through his tinted windshield! how manfully he splatters his gold-plated spittoon! how resourcefully he takes a beer from his built-in refrigerator!"

So numerous were the luxuries in the pickup that many owners were unable to cope with the bewildering contradictions that ensued. Dr. Ft. Stockton Miranda, a psychologist who counseled over two hundred pickup owners in the Lindisfarne area in 1964-65, recalls, "It was an extremely dangerous situation. Consider: here is a cowboy. The world nurses an immutable image of him as gaunt, deprived, weather-beaten, heroic. He is, every waking moment, acutely conscious of this stereotype. Yet he spends ninety-five percent of those waking moments in coil-springed, easy-chair opulence, the very air he breathes so carefully modulated that from January to December he neither sweats nor shivers; he is more pampered than a baby in its crib. He sees his predicament clearly: he wants to be what the world thinks he is; yet once he has tasted the luxuries, he cannot think of, cannot even remotely consider giving them up. This ironic dichotomy between stereotype and fact produced an extreme defensive belligerence among many Texas Occident pickup owners. It was so intense that today it is difficult to imagine."

Yet many took the contradiction in stride, shaking their heads with rueful amusement when they were joshed about their wheeled epicurism. A Texas A&M sociologist who delivered a humorous lecture on the topic at the Lindisfarne Lyceum in February 1965 received warm applause, and he was not shot until an hour later as he returned to his hotel.

The first attempts to reconcile Wild West image with pickup fact were cosmetic, as indeed have been almost all others since. Always alert to sentiment in the Occident, Ford introduced the Posse 250 NG with non-glare glass in October 1966, claiming "no one can tell, not even from five feet away, that your windows are rolled up and the air conditioner on." Non-glare glass in the windshield was offered as an option "to those rugged men who in the best Texas Occidental tradition wish to seem eyeball to eyeball with the savage elements, the searing summer dust of the Big Bend, the stinging sleet and brutal northers of the high plains."

Chevrolet countered four months later with the Sac and Fox 251 NG-E and 251 NG-EE, which, along with non-glare glass standard in the windshield and all windows, featured a simulated denim-clad elbow resting on the left window or, on the 251 NG-EE, both left and right windows. Despite the success of its cologned waterseat model, Dodge suddenly found itself far behind the Posse and Sac and Fox sales. It regained a portion of the market in Spring 1967 with its MGR, which had a mahogany gun rack, and that summer its sales shot up with the .30-.30 MGR, which had a simulated rifle on the gun rack. Ford retaliated with the 2R-1TS-GR (two simulated rifles, one with telescopic sight), and that fall Chevrolet brought out its 3TSR-HBHB (three simulated rifles with telescopic sights, a hanging bandolier and holster belt), with options for a simulated .30 caliber machine gun and a bazooka, and Dodge found itself further behind than ever. In 1968, however, Dodge correctly gauged the diametrically opposed thrusts of the Occidental pickup market—that is, to drive vehicles which seemed more and more rugged and rustic while they became posher and posher—and turned the tables with its Llama 252 PD, which had a pre-dented right front fender.

Reeling from this coup, Chevrolet and Ford struck back in 1970 with the Sac and Fox 253 PDD (two dents) and the Posse 254 PDDD (three dents). GMC joined the fray the following year with the PMS-DDDD (permanently mud-stained, four dents). In 1973 Dodge introduced the Llama 254 PDR (pre-dented and rolled), and by 1976 all pickups sold were PDRs.

Amid charges and counter-charges ranging from imitation to outright industrial theft, Ford and Chevrolet stunned the 1977 market with the Posse 255 PDR-LB, featuring the shape of a leaping buck deer smashed into the front end, an antler jutting from the right front headlamp, and the Sac and Fox 256 PDR-SB, which had black buzzard feathers encircling a bright red oval beginning above the grill and extending over the hood to the windshield. For reasons analysts have never agreed upon, however, neither model fulfilled or even approximated the high sales predicted by their makers, and production of both was halted in early 1978.

By then Dodge had introduced its 257 PDR-PMTS (pre-dented and rolled, permanently mud- and tobacco-stained), and Ford and Chevrolet scrambled desperately to repair the damage of the Leaping Buck and Splattered Buzzard fiascos. Recalling Studebaker's catastrophically premature PC model of nearly a quarter century earlier, Chevrolet decided the time for pre-canned pickups had finally arrived. The Sac and Fox 258 PDR-PMS-RCC, with a rusted Coors can welded squarely in the middle of the bed, arrived in Lindisfarne in October 1978 and was quickly followed by the PSSCC (permanent stainless steel Coors can) model in December. Ford countered in February 1979 with the C-LS (one Coors, one Lone Star), and the following October Dodge brought out the state-of-the-art LSLSU-CDF (two Lone Stars up, one Coors down and flattened), which has been copied by all others since.

Little change has occurred in pickup design in the ensuing years. Dodge inaugurated the self-scouring spittoon in late 1979, and was quickly copied by the other manufacturers. Chevrolet, in response to the continuing anguish of many owners over the contradiction between their cherished frontier image and their equally cherished luxury, introduced the ill-fated Sac and Fox 259-NS-NAC-CIS-CCS (no springs, no air conditioner, cast iron seat, coffee can spittoon) in 1981. Advertisements in the *Gatherer* discussed frankly the "hypocrisy which many have practiced, however unwillingly," and offered the NS-NAC-CIS-CCS as "a viable, straightforward answer to the problem in the best tradition of the Occident. In this vehicle you will be incontestably uncomfortable; you will, in fact, suffer, and over a period of years, almost certainly incur spinal damage. But no one—*no one*—will be able to say you didn't rough it."

Buyers "agonized and postponed their decisions for months, suspended between the soft life they wanted and what they knew was right. In the end they chose to be upholstered, refrigerated, and wrong," the August 11, 1981 *Gatherer* reported. And the NS-NAC-CIS failed.

Only the PD (permanent dog) innovations have had any impact since then. Dodge brought out its badly conceived LGSCB (Live German Shepherd chained in the pickup bed) in 1982 but, more correctly sensing the market, then followed in early 1983 with its PMGSB (permanent mechanical German Shepherd in the pickup bed), an authentic-looking facsimile which barked continuously when the engine was running. Ford and Chevrolet followed suit with PMBD and PMLD (permanent mechanical barking, lunging dogs) models in 1984, Ford's PMLDs featuring an electric-eye-actuated mechanical Doberman Pinscher which snarled and lunged at passers-by in parking lots,

Chevrolet's a mechanical pit bull which crouched, snarled, and lunged in a random circular pattern when the engine was running. Dodge brought out its Japanese-designed PMASDBCR (permanent mechanical Australian Sheepdog balanced on cab roof) in 1985.

Stung and re-stung by the incessant barbs thrown by the *Gatherer* over the decades, the Pickup Owners of Occidental Texas Association has made occasional attempts to refurbish its image. Following a June 1977 editorial in which the *Gatherer* alleged that "less than three percent of all drivers can park their clumsy, unnavigable, and half-created pickups in an average parking space, and even fewer pretend to try. And now, with the new cab-and-a-halfs, king cabs, double and triple cabs, it is a virtual miracle to find a pickup parked in fewer than three spaces," POOTA retaliated with a full-page advertisement asserting the pickup's unwieldy characteristics were, "in reality, a stern test of driving skill which every pickup driver gladly accepts and successfully passes."

A "Pickupoadeo" was proclaimed so that "the doubting public may see, once and for all, how finely honed are our skills." But as the *Gatherer* gleefully reported, "only seven pickups out of the entire Texas Occident showed up, and after a few abortive attempts to accomplish the first test, a simple maneuverability run, all folded their tents and went home."

In the summer of 1982 Jay Bart Brad Shumacher, the impish younger brother of Arturo V, took a secret survey of the cowboys on the sprawling Shumacher Ranch, asking them what mode of transportation they preferred. Thirteen responded that they wanted ten-speed bicycles for work around the ranch; four said they would stick to horses; the other three voted for a motor scooter, a small motorbike, and a dune buggy, respectively. For trips into town, eleven still preferred bicycles, the same four voted for horses, and five named Mopeds. For longer trips, all but the horsemen were unanimous: "Give us some small, agile, economic four-cylinder car," Bob Tom Hernandez pleaded, and Rio Colorado Herrenmeyer apparently spoke for the majority when he said wistfully, "A little Honda Civic would be ideal; if it has to be something larger, make it a Volkswagen bus."

Confronted with the results, Arturo V called a meeting of the ranch-hands after the fall roundup. "I'm going to replace most of our vehicles this winter," he said; "I've seen the survey Jay Bart Brad took, and I believe it is valid, because I also have talked privately with many of you, and you have told me basically the same thing. I myself feel as you do: it's time to get rid of these damned pickups."

A murmur of assent passed among the cowboys.

"So now is your chance," Arturo said. "Rio Colorado, you voted for a Moped and a Honda Civic. Think about the colors you want, and I'll order them tomorrow. Bob Tom, you said a ten-speed and—"

"Arturo, could you hold on just a little bit?" Rio Colorado asked. He looked anxiously around the bunkhouse at the others. "I been think-ing: would you mind just getting me one of them new beat-up Chevy pickups?"

Pencil suspended over his clipboard, Arturo stared at the cowboy.

"With the automatic dog and the beer cans in the back," Rio Colorado stammered.

Bob Tom scuffed the toe of his boot on the floor and said without looking up, "I reckon maybe that's what I want too."

"We are washing our hands of this muddle," the *Gatherer* sneered when the story leaked out in February 1983. "This is our last editorial on the subject. People drive pickups—these clumsy, ludicrous visual and aural pollutants—not because they want to but because of what they mistakenly feel to be relentless peer pressure. They are trapped forever in a vicious tradition that sustains itself on the despair and self-deception of its victims."

COWBOY BELT BUCKLE

The cowboy belt buckle, or omphalos, as it is commonly known in the Texas Occident, has changed radically in form and function since the early days when it was used primarily as a means of protection. The buckle, of course, has been constantly evolving since Medieval times, for it is all that remains of the suit of armor that once covered knights, the cowboys of another age, from head to toe. As gunpowder came into general use, armor gradually shrank to decorative head and torso covering in the seventeenth and eighteenth centuries, and finally simply to the large belt buckle which has been favored most of the time in the Texas Occident for the last 150 years.

Not surprisingly, the last full suits of armor actually used on a daily basis in the United States were those worn in the nineteenth century by a few cowboys on the Shumacher Ranch, where ancient traditions died harder than anywhere else. All but one of those cowboys had given up the practice because of the attendant inconveniences—rust, heatstroke, and frequent stampedes caused by the creaking, flashing armor—by 1890. The lone exception was Roberto Slape, one of the seven barefoot Slape brothers, who clung to his graceful, gleaming lightweight steel-plate armor until 1905, when he was struck by lightning.

For the less eccentric cowboys in the Occident, the buckle functioned as a protective device well into the twentieth century. As has been demonstrated in many movies, sixgun-wielding outlaws and inlaws alike have scrupulously adhered to the Code of the West when shooting their friends and enemies, aiming always at the belt buckle. The cliché which is still popular today, "Buckle up for safety," in fact, originated in the Texas Occident in the 1850's and 60's, where there were few bullet-scarred cowboys and even fewer killings, but one could hardly find a belt buckle anywhere which had not been pocked by half a dozen bullets. In those days, the accuracy of the gun-toters in the Occident could be easily calculated, year by year, according to the size of the belt buckle: the smaller the buckles, the more the cowboys trusted each other's aim. It is generally agreed that 1858 marked the zenith of good marksmanship in the Occident. That was the year when the Bullet Buckle, a saucer-shaped buckle no larger than a dime, was popular.

Ironically, the strong religious beliefs of many cowboys in the Occident resulted in several deaths in the years before 1869, when the Toxbox, or Texas Occident Box Holster, came into general use and eliminated most of the danger of gunfighting. As is generally known by readers of Western novels, the Bible carried in a shirt pocket is, like the buckle, a traditional target in gunfights. On a number of occasions in 1866-68, gunfighters faced the dilemma of which to shoot at, the Bible or the buckle. Crease Perkins, the son of the well-known Kalplish Ranch wrangler Hurley Perkins and one of the last cowboys to die in a gunfight in the Occident, wore a Bullet Buckle and also carried a copy of the Tyndale New Testament in his shirt pocket. He was killed by Rodolfo Slape, another of the seven barefoot Slape brothers, in front of the Sotol Saloon in Lindisfarne after a dispute over a chess game. It was a gunfight which no one would have expected to produce bloodshed, for Rodolfo Slape, unlike his brothers, was a crack shot. He aimed at Perkins' belt buckle, but as he squeezed the trigger he realized that Crease was carrying a Bible and would doubtless prefer to be shot in it. He tried to shift his aim to the Bible just as he shot, and hit Perkins between buckle and Bible.

A conference of the Texas Occident Society against Plugging Each Other solved the problem shortly thereafter with the invention of a compartment within the buckle which could hold a Bible, if its wearer

desired to carry one. The device was known as the Bible Belt. A larger version of the same buckle was developed by Carrasco van Deventer, a cowboy on the Shumacher Ranch, for carrying a measure of rolled oats to share with his horse. It was called the Grain Belt.

Although the size and shape of the cowboy belt buckle in the Occident has varied with each generation in the twentieth century, the general trend has always been toward a larger buckle. This preference has been encouraged by the desire of many cowboys to display quotations on their buckles so that the accumulated wisdom of the human race may be conveyed to others (Conveyer Belt). Long excerpts from the works of Boethius, Pico della Mirandola, Tolstoy, and Louis L'Amour have been the most popular. The quotes are sometimes printed in reverse so that a cowboy, if he has the good luck to encounter a pool of clear water during his long, lonely hours on the range, may refresh himself intellectually by reading his reflected buckle.

Cowboys have always been fickle about buckle styles from one season to the next, and more than one retailer in the Occident has been caught with unsellable buckles. When Betsy Hubschrauber I, the resourceful owner of Hubschrauber's General Store in Lindisfarne, found that she could not sell a consignment of 500 buckles which featured an illustrated rendition of Spenser's famous sixteenth-century poem *Epithalamion*, she moved them to the housewares department, turned them over, and sold them as dinner plates.

Stricter security measures at airports have proven to be incompatible with cowboy belt buckles, which, when they are worn near metal detectors, set off bells and sirens and bring guards waving guns. As a result it is not unusual at the Lindisfarne and Midland-Odessa airports to see long lines of embarrassed cowboys holding up their jeans while they wait for their belts to be returned.

The practice of awarding huge silver or silver-inlaid-with-gold buckles as trophies at rodeos has had one interesting side effect in the Occident. At Sul Ross State University in Alpine, many of the students majoring in Range Animal Science are rodeo champions and therefore wear belts, called Sun Belts, with the big buckles on them. As a result, the professors there often teach class wearing sunglasses or even welding goggles to avoid being blinded by the phalanx of glittering buckles confronting them.

The real evolution of the cowboy belt buckle in the past century, however, has been not in its shape or size but in its emergence as a central symbol of philosophical thought in the Texas Occident. This fact should come as no surprise to anyone familiar with the daily life of a cowboy. In his solitude and close communion with the purest and freest of nature, the cowboy has had ample opportunity to sort out the complexities of life and formulate a clear, coherent understanding of both the phenomenal and noumenal worlds. As he has done so, he has come to perceive the belt and its buckle as having a far more important function than holding up his pants.

It is perhaps also not surprising that Miguel Cervantes, the aged philosopher-foreman of the Kalplish Ranch, has had much to say about the philosophical implications of the cowboy belt buckle. A recent letter written by Cervantes to the Texas Folklore Society, which relies heavily on Cervantes' vast accumulation of knowledge about the Occident, illustrates his concern and interest:

"It is no accident that we cowboys lean against the corral or pose for photographers during the daily photo sessions with our thumbs hooked in our belt on each side of the buckle, or, in the case of some generously bellied ranchers, with one or both hands securely gripping the buckle itself under the planetary stomach bulge," Cervantes wrote. "Our thumbs point toward the buckle, or omphalos, as we prefer to call it, and our fingers ray out in all directions of the compass from the omphalos because we regard it as the focal point, the center of the known universe, and the belt as the symbolic equator.

"In our daily lives the desert is either hot or cold, one or the other, never in-between; similarly, we experience the dichotomies of dawn and dusk, day and night, male and female, land and sky, wet and dry (though more often dry than wet), truth and falsehood (though more often truth, for cowboys know not how to lie), good and evil, and life and death. The belt symbolically divides man as we see all else divided. Never mind which half is good and which evil; the point is the division. But the omphalos rules the belt and symbolizes a hope for reconciliation and fusion of these many opposites. The omphalos is thus the symbolic navel, the wellspring of our lives.

"Accordingly, we see these damned leisure suits which so-called men are wearing these days as amoral, if not downright immoral. They have no belts, and worse, no buckles, and are part pants and part shirt and neither one at the same time, and so they blur the distinction between the two halves of things. They ought to be banned forever.

"We are well aware of the contemporary notion of no absolute good or evil, and we have our own instances of it. Pickup IV, for example, was the wickedest cow that ever lived, yet she shared with many of us who knew her a profound appreciation for the very best in barbed wire sculpture—even as she was running through the fence and tearing it all to thunder for half a mile.

"On balance, however, no matter how praiseworthy her esthetic inclinations, she was still an ornery damned cow. In the long haul a cow, or anything else, is one or the other, good or bad, and she was bad. And when a man crawls out of his bedroll in the morning he ought to know whether the thing he's putting on is his pants or his shirt, and he shouldn't fool with some baby-romper compromise that will knock his philosophical apperceptions cattywhompus the whole blamed day."

So the omphalos remains today as both the anatomical and philosophical focus of the cowboy's being. Small wonder that nine out of ten cowboys go to bed wearing not only their hats but their belts, that they always go to sleep with their thumbs securely hooked on each side of that center of centers, the buckle, that they all want to be buried the same way in the Texas Occident, and that they all swear by Macleoud's Thumb-rot Balm.

HORSE AND SADDLE

The love affair between the cowboy and his horse in the Texas Occident, and in the American West in general, has been celebrated in song and story for well over a century, but it is exemplified nowhere so well as in the starkly tragic tale of Yolanda Hubschrauber, which has been passed down in the Occident from one generation of embittered wives and spinsters to the next.

The shy, lovely young girl who became the legendary Yolanda Yuccaseed, the

> image of rue
> plumb-bob true,

as the poet Raul Carew put it, was the daughter of Udo Hubschrauber, the owner of a prosperous but ill-fated windmill in Lindisfarne, and she was the older sister of Betsy Hubschrauber I, who became one of Lindisfarne's most prominent citizens.

As her story begins, we see Yolanda leaning out over the porch railing of her father's windmill, which is both mill and house. Her hands are clasped over her bosom. Before her stands Numero Herrenmeyer, a dashing, handsome young cowboy from the Shumacher Ranch. His graceful horse waits beside him. Numero looks at his horse, then at Yolanda. Her auburn hair hangs in a long, heavy braid down the back of her best gingham dress, the one with the blue ruffles, and she is beautiful—by human standards. The cowboy looks at his sloe-eyed, sleekly curved horse again. It whinnies impatiently and tosses its silken mane in the twilight. Numero looks at Yolanda. She cannot whinny. His decision made, the cowboy mounts up and rides off into the gloaming, leaving the girl forever. Yolanda crumples over the porch railing with a broken heart.

The details have been chronicled many times of how, in the years that followed, Yolanda turned in despair to the desert of the Texas Occident, identifying its desolation with the barrenness dominating her soul because of Numero Herrenmeyer's perfidy. She began to scatter mesquite and yucca seeds across the Occident in a desperate, lifelong, and perhaps life-sustaining belief that greening up the rock-strewn slopes and moonscape plains would somehow green up the wastelands of her own heart. Whether she succeeded in the latter is not known, but she did succeed in covering thousands of square miles of the Occident with mesquite and yucca.

Old-timers today speak of Yolanda Yuccaseed as a gaunt, bent, leathery old woman in a gingham dress, her long white braid flying behind her as she strode urgently, always urgently, across the desert toward some ever-receding destination. She was the loneliest, most melancholy figure the Occident has ever known, and the archetypal victim of the Occident cowboys' perverse love for their horses.

"The problem is not new, nor is it unique to the Occident," Miguel Cervantes, the philosopher-foreman of the Kalplish Ranch, wrote in a letter to the Lindisfarne *Weekly Gatherer* in 1868. "Why do you think the knights of medieval times encased themselves in suits of metal from head to toe? Certainly not to protect themselves, for they were not cowards. They would have preferred to do battle *au naturel*, like the fighters we see depicted by Greek statues. Nay, these crusaders were the defenders of high morality: they wore armor to separate themselves from the warm and vibrant skin, the—Yes, I will say it!—rippling, supple musculature of their horses. And today, if we cannot hold ourselves aloof from our alluring steeds with chaps of iron and jeans of chain mail, then we must find other but equally effective means."

One of many solutions, none satisfactory, to the delicate and perplexing problem was offered by Hurley Perkins, the Kalplish Ranch wrangler who often collaborated with Miguel Cervantes in dealing with the ethical dilemmas of the Occident. He founded the Texas Occident Bucking School in 1869, an always-controversial institution which, Cervantes wrote many years later, "Everybody despised, Hurley most especially, and yet everybody used because we couldn't, and still can't, think of anything better."

The unhappy purpose of the bucking school was to cause men to dislike their horses. In other words, it taught young horses, and older ones too if they wandered in from the wild and desired to participate in the work of the ranch, to buck: to buck off their riders, to bite and kick them at every opportunity, to roll with them in cactus or buffalo wallows, or to knock them off by running under low-hanging branches or scraping against boulders.

"It was the sorriest, contrariest work imaginable," Cervantes wrote. "The horse is the sweetest, most loving, most dutiful creature that ever existed. The horse wants nothing more than a human master on whom it can lavish affection. Breathes there a horse anywhere that would not prefer a harsh, cold, filthy iron bit in its mouth on a freezing winter morning to a bucket of sweetened rolled oats in a warm stable? No, nowhere. Breathes there a horse anywhere that would not prefer being spurred and flailed, unwatered and unfed, through blistering heat and choking dust till it drops of exhaustion to spring days of green buffalo grass and clover on a sunny hillside? No, nowhere. Yet we sent our bewildered colts, who wanted nothing more than to slave night and day for some demanding master until they were too old for anything except coyote bait, to bucking school. There they were taught all that was against their natures; they were taught to run away when their beloved masters appeared with rope or halter; to step on toes; to leap sideways when a would-be rider, swinging onto the horse, was in the most awkward position; to lull their rider into feeling secure, then throw him into a barbed-wire fence; to step into imaginary prairie dog holes; to slip from narrow mountain trails; to shy unexpectedly and violently from rabbits, yucca blooms, or nothing at all. Little wonder that it was almost impossible to hire someone to work at the bucking school, or that Hurley Perkins himself was twice prevented from committing suicide in 1876 and again in 1878."

Yet none of this was enough. Cowboys still loved their horses, and all over the Occident one might see young women in their best gingham dresses swooned in despair over their porch railings.

The situation became so desperate that, in 1880, the Texas Occident turned to the saddle as a remedy.

Cowboys, of course, prefer to ride their horses bareback. The underground literary magazines of the Occident are filled with juvenile rhapsodies about the practice.

"We rode into McKinley Canyon, Alastair and I," one writer tells us. "I was barefoot, naturally, and my toes reveled in some warm, still unshed patches of Alastair's winter coat. Alastair wore neither bridle nor halter, and we wandered where we would, sometimes on the path, sometimes into the creek, sometimes up the steep slope to the left when we wanted to investigate a fallen log or the song of some feathered creature. The mountainside was rainbowed with the first spring flowers, and I had woven dozens of the delicate blooms—Jill o' the rock, angelflutes, starhorns, Texas Edelweiss—into Alastair's mane. At times I, by the slightest touch of my fingertips on the horse's lustrous neck, indicated a direction, but usually Alastair, divining my least inclination before I knew what I wanted, had already taken the initiative. At noon, just after we had shared a tuna sandwich and a hatful of water which I had dipped from a cold, clear pool, we saw the stray steers which we had been sent to round up. Alastair cocked one ear forward and looked at me questioningly, not wanting to break the mood but ready to spring into action if I so decided. Stroking the horse's velvet nose, I gazed for a moment up the canyon wall to where a mockingbird scolded from atop a live oak. Then I shook my head. 'The day is too perfect,' I said. Alastair nodded, smiling."

The first saddles were sold in Macleoud's Bootshop in Lindisfarne. Since the ranchers and cowboys did not want to burden their beloved horses with an ounce more weight than necessary, they commissioned Angus Macleoud to make lightweight English saddles. It was, they soon realized, a grievous error.

"We hated them from the first day," Cervantes wrote. "They were disgustingly ugly. Many cowboys likened them to burnt tortillas. It was their miserly frugality that repelled us most. Their servile pommel, their stingy, merely functional cantle and skirt, and their plainly parsimonious flap and knee roll were insults both to the beauty and the sensitivity of our horses. For while a horse will gladly endure the most repugnant colors and shapes for its master's sake, the fact is that the horse has exquisite taste, far better than humans, and nothing saddens it more than to be intimately associated with an object that is offensive in conception and form. The hideousness of the English saddle, we felt, surely was a basic reason for the moral decay of that nation. We quickly determined that our horses, who deserved so much better, would have better saddles, saddles that enhanced not only their beauty but the quality of their lives."

The fledgling saddlemakers of the Occident had close at hand, of course, a model far more to their taste in the Moorish saddle, as modified in Mexico and used by the vaqueros. Ranchers and cowboys alike loved the nobly aquiline horn, the tiered-leather rosettes, rose-knot whangs, braided latigos, and meticulously engraved sudaderos of the Moorish saddles. Soon many horses were crossing the desert in concha-bejeweled splendor. For the truth was that while horses were generally purists in taste, preferring the simple and unprepossessing in ornament and dress, even the most modest among them could not help arching their necks and prancing a little when they were decked out in a richly burnished mahogany saddle all aglitter with silver and elaborate carvings.

By 1885 every saddlemaker had turned away from the English saddle, and not a single one was being produced in the Occident. Concha shops sprang up as the demand for original designs skyrocketed. Cowboys and horses alike quickly learned to prefer hand-worked conchas, and by 1890 it was generally agreed that the surest way to turn a proud, high-spirited horse into a lumpish, sullen, swaybacked nag was to decorate its saddle with mass-produced conchas. Many of the shops quickly began to specialize, and there were vociferous adherents of various designs, from simple four- to eight-point stars to monarch butterflies, hearts inlaid with gold, Celtic crosses, and numerous shapes taken from cabalistic and gnostic systems of symbolism.

Similarly, the leather of the saddle became more and more elaborately decorated and esthetically more ambitious, evolving from repetitious embossed, or stamped, patterns such as the poco oak, paisley, California rose, basketweave, Ryon floral, Macleoud herringbone, and sotol treble clef to carved reliefs. These, in turn, changed quickly from traditional patterns to original sculptures, and thus to true art.

The apogee of this genre was reached in 1891 by Ramon Slape, one of the seven barefoot Slape brothers, with the completion of his epic, intricately detailed *Cabora Creek Stampede Fenders*. It was carved, ironically enough, on a saddle for Numero Herrenmeyer, the cowboy from the Shumacher Ranch who broke Yolanda Hubschrauber's heart. The work depicted a famous stampede of 20,000 Longhorn and Spiny Angus cows which occurred on the Kalplish Ranch in 1858.

"It is equally classical and romantic, with something oddly rococoist echoing in the curvature of the cows' horns," Hurley Perkins wrote in a review published in the Lindisfarne *Weekly Gatherer* in 1892. "It has marvelous depth and detail, the expression on the face of every cow being individual and unique. Old-timers from this area will instantly recognize, as I did, many of the cows in the carving. In a cursory inspection the first time I saw it, in fact, I identified and correctly named over 800 head. You can well understand that I shed not a few tears, for it was an unexpected reunion with a great many long-gone friends. These saddle fenders are readily comparable to Ghiberti's 'Gates of Paradise', and may well eclipse them."

Numero Herrenmeyer never sat in the saddle Ramon Slape carved for him, although he used it on his favorite horses—Medusa's Muse,

Mesopotamia, and Uncle Bill, among others—for several decades. Rather than scratch or wear out the carving, he sat behind the saddle on his horse's rump. His reverence for the saddle finally led to his death in 1924, when he was caught in a freezing rainstorm. As was his custom, he threw his slicker over his treasured saddle. He arrived at the home corral encrusted in a half-inch of ice and died six days later of pneumonia. His saddle is now a part of the permanent collection at the Texas Occident Museum of Fine Arts in Lindisfarne, although its inclusion was loudly protested by WAH, the Occident chapter of Women Against Horses.

In their frantic desire to achieve depth and three-dimensonality, and to match Slape's achievement, saddle carvers experimented with ever thicker, more exotic leathers in the mid 1880's—water buffalo, hippo, rhinoceros, and even elephant. Finally, at a Texas Occident Carvers Conference in April 1897, Ramon Slape himself brought the mad competition to an end by calling for carvers to use a multi-media approach. In so doing, they set a course which, in its essential principles, has not swerved to this day.

"Leave the rhinos and elephants alone," Slape said in a keynote speech. "Let us kill nothing. Let us use only bullhide from bulls who have died of old age for our saddles. Instead of seeking depth with our carving knives, let us reach it with paint, with color. Instead of cutting into the leather, let us build upon it with plaster and papier-mâché."

Since then, for better or worse, saddle art has reflected the concerns of the art world, and of the world in general. If any influence has held more sway than others, it has been that of the French Impressionists, for saddle artists have returned many times to the sunbursts and bright blues of Van Gogh and to the delicate leafy greens and red-orange flowers of Monet. Saddles have been covered with alligator, llama, polar bear, and anteater skin, and saddlebags of angora and ermine have been common. The flamboyant Arturo Shumacher II, of the Shumacher Ranch, once had a saddle inlaid with so much gold and silver that it had to be carried in a pickup alongside his horse. During World War II saddles often were painted olive drab, or in abstract camouflage colors. Pommels were carved in the shapes of popular warplanes such as the P-38. Mink-hair lariats enjoyed a brief vogue in 1947, and saddles were festooned with innumerable wooden beads in the early Seventies.

Perhaps the most forgettable period was the glittery mid-Fifties. During this time saddlebags, cantles, fenders, and girths were often brilliantly outlined with flashing neon lights.

"I hate it when we get caught out after dark," Tad Kalplish II grumbled to the *Weekly Gatherer* in 1959; "it looks more like Times Square than a roundup."

A similar period of faddish nonsense led—for a short time, thankfully—to the modification and introduction of the howdah, the canopied seat used for riding elephants and sometimes camels. Called "howdies" in the Occident, a seat was raised on slender aluminum legs above the saddle on the horse so the rider would not damage the complex shapes and figures sculpted onto the saddle.

The howdy was met with quick derision.

"Nothing—nothing in this world—looks so stupid as someone precariously perched on a swaying chair eight feet above his horse's back," the *Weekly Gatherer* observed. "These idiots look more like streetlamps, or canaries in a cage, than cowboys."

So the howdy disappeared, although, oddly enough, it remained long enough to be seen by deer and antelope hunters from Dallas and Houston, who immediately demanded that howdies be installed on their jeeps. Thus one may still see howdies swarming all over the Occident each fall. "The occupant of the chair," the *Gatherer* commented, "if he is not falling out or shooting himself, sits there with all the dignity and intelligence of a boiled penguin."

The new electronic technology of the Seventies and Eighties has been welcomed by the horsemen of the Texas Occident, for now all horses enjoy air-conditioned saddle blankets, eliminating much of the uncomfortable perspiration of the past. Compact cassette tape players have enabled cowboys to throw away the bulky guitars, violins, saxophones, and

instruments with which they had been entertaining their music-loving horses for many decades. By 1986, according to an article in the *Gatherer*, eighty-eight percent of the cowboys in the Occident had cassette players built into the pommels of their saddles, with rear speakers in the cantles.

"From San Angelo to El Paso, the typical roundup is now a cacophony of classical music, hard rock, and jazz blaring from a dozen pommels," the *Gatherer* article sneered. "And of course there are always a few depraved horses who will listen to nothing but 'Mule Train' from dawn till dusk."

"Cacophony or not," Miguel Cervantes, the aging foreman of the Kalplish Ranch, retorted in a letter to the editor the following week, "it beats hell out of trying to play a bass viol while you're roping a calf."

The basic problem that faced the Occident over a hundred years ago, of course, remains today: ranchers and cowboys are still in love with their horses. The truth is that, however laudable the intent of those who introduced it in the Occident, the saddle—that useless, tawdry, over-adorned thin bit of insulation—is no more effective than the purdah in India, or bundling in New England. For proof, one need look no further than the range graffiti which abound in the Texas Occident. The following untitled poem, which was laboriously spelled out with piled rocks over a five-acre plot on the Merton Ranch, is typical:

Why do I
Clean the frog of your foot
With more care than the vamp of my boot?
Comb your flaxen mane
With more care than my linens (had I the same)?
Adore your hooves and hocks
More than whisky and gold, and clocks?

Cause your beauty and grace
Mean more to me than the ace

Of spades; because your horsehood . . .
[Line obliterated by flash flood] . . .
Whether on hill or in stall,
These virtues hold me happy in thrall.

Similarly, a fragment discovered on Schooner Rock near the north branch of Cabora Creek on the Kalplish Ranch has been attributed to Raul "One-rhyme" Carew, the Texas Occident poet whose work was so disliked during his lifetime that he could find no publisher. He was reduced to carving his poems clandestinely on boulders in the desert.

A Cowboy's Apology to His Horse
While Saddling Same

Kindly forgive me O cayuse so true,
For these pond'rous burthens, their weight so undue—
For this massive saddle held together with glue,
This rope, and slicker, and blanket blue,
Six cans of beans, and a bottle too;
Ten pounds of coffee and a lantern new,
A big thick book that I borrowed from Lou,
A rocking chair and a jar of tofu;
For snaffles and martingale and reins numb'ring two,
Cruppers and girths and nails in your shoe,
Throatlatch and surcingle . . .
[illegible] . . . in the world anew,
I'll be the horse, and you the buckaroo.

The wives and girlfriends, or would-be wives and girlfriends, of these cowboys with strayed affections suffer as much as ever, and if anything, are even more resentful than ever, for a century of playing second fiddle to horses has exacerbated their tempers and sharpened their tongues. The Texas Occident Bucking School, which is still in operation under the direction of Jesus Perkins, the great-grandson of its founder, Hurley Perkins, is the constant target of the women of the Occident, who say that it is wholly ineffective. It has been the scene of violent demonstrations by women who suspect that, despite its professed purpose, it is really a crude excuse for men to spend yet more time with their horses.

A recent incident involving Betsy Hubschrauber IV illustrates the point. Betsy IV, who had heard the story of her unfortunate great-aunt, Yolanda, hundreds of times in her childhood, was acutely conscious of the horse as a Texas Occident girl's most formidable rival. But Maury Sutter, one of the Occident's finest knobiters, had sworn to Betsy IV on their wedding day that he loved her and only her, and no one else, not even his favorite horse, Descartes. Five months after their wedding, Betsy IV was driving home from Lindisfarne in Maury's pickup when one of the tires blew out. As she crawled under the rear of the vehicle to get the spare tire she saw, freshly and boldly scratched on a shock absorber,

I ♥ *Descartes.*

She changed the tire, went home, and started to do her household chores as usual. But as she began to dice mushrooms, onions, and green peppers for supper she worked more and more slowly. Looking out the kitchen window toward Ordnance Butte, she saw Maury, riding Descartes, emerge from a grove of mesquites planted by her great-aunt Yolanda a century earlier. Suddenly Betsy IV clenched her fists and screamed. Who can say what thoughts raced through her head then, what long, insistent call of blood and kinship and gender loyalty she heard, what tipped the balance and caused her to extract a measure of vengeance for her ancestor's decades of suffering? At any rate, that same evening she substituted poisonous toadstools for the mushrooms in Maury and Descartes' favorite quiche. An all-female jury in Lindisfarne acquitted her in November 1988.

LARIATS AND LASSOING

Little more is known about the true importance of the lariat in the Texas Occident today than a century ago. Whether, as some Occident observers have alleged, the lariat is used by cowboys in a meditative practice which is similar to that of some Eastern religions, but which developed much later and entirely independently, has not been proven, or disproven.

Several facts, however, most of them contrary to popular belief, are known and beyond dispute. One is that the lariat is *not* used and has never been used to rope cattle—to snare them, hold them captive, or bind them in any way.

"You can blame this nonsensical misinformation on the rodeo crowd, most of whom are from places like Ohio and Connecticut," Miguel Cervantes, the foreman of the Kalplish Ranch, told a *New York Times* reporter in 1910. "They collected all these deranged animals, you see—paranoid calves that run away from humans, and bulls and horses that have been trained to buck off their riders, or tormented till they do. The derangement spread to the people involved, for violence begets violence. The first thing we knew, they were roping calves and flipping them end over end. Sometimes they broke the poor beasts' necks. And then, to justify their inhumanity, they pretended we did that sort of thing as part of our everyday work on the ranches in the Occident, which is a blatant lie. We'd as soon rope our grandmothers. Sooner, in fact."

Unfortunately, thanks to heavy pressure exerted by the powerful rodeo lobby, that *Times* interview with Cervantes was never published.

It is also known that the first uses of the lariat, or *strand*, as it is often called in the Occident, were decorative. Just as a cowboy might give his girlfriend a strand of pearls, he gave his horse a strand of brightly colored lariat. The gifts were so similar in the meaning and spirit with which they were given, in fact, that cowboys often confused them and gave pearls to their horses and ropes to their girlfriends or wives—and occasionally still do so today.

The first lariats were about four feet long—just long enough to loop around and adorn a horse's neck. In the beginning, they were dyed in bright colors—orange and magenta were favorites—and patterns of spiraling stripes became popular, along with polka dots and checks. Horses soon realized that ropes were available in many exotic braids, and it was a humble horse indeed who wore only a rawhide reata or a fiber twist rope and did not have at least a few strands of pyramid braid, Sussex double floral, or Arapahoe loop-on-loop. In the 1980's, however, the trend has been toward subtler colors, metallic gray and antique green among them. Ironically, many horses today favor the simpler understatement of twisted fiber lariats in their natural colors.

As cowboys became bolder and more lavish in showing their affection, additional strands were added, and various baubles—silver bells, conchas, marbles, glass beads, feathers, pocket watches, cougar and bear teeth and claws, javelina tusks, coins, flags, arrowheads, rattlesnake rattles, dice, Christmas ornaments, cut geodes, and gemstones were attached to the rope until some cowboys began to ridicule the extravagance.

"They look more like a blamed bunch of curio shops than horses," Valentine Finch, the Shumacher Ranch foreman, wrote in a letter to the Lindisfarne *Weekly Gatherer* in 1875. "When they trot they sound like a tinker's wagon coming."

Horses became quite vain about the number of strands their cowboy-admirer-owners gave them, and for a time an envious, unhealthy status-seeking competition developed among them, with some horses wearing so many strands that they looked like mummies and could scarcely walk. The idiom, "stranded on a desert island," in fact, is a descendant of the original saying in the Occident, "stranded in the desert," which referred to a conceited horse so heavily encumbered with decorative strand, or lariat, that he might die of thirst before he reached a water tank. Conversely, "Don't dally with me," the warning in the popular song, originated among those horses in the Occident whose stingy owners gave them only a *dally*, a single short strand of rope looped around the saddle horn with a half-hitch knot.

Most of the facts about the real significance of the lariat in the Texas Occident remain shrouded in mystery, and close-mouthed cowboys have, for many decades, steadfastly refused to discuss the matter. Enough is now known, however, to make it seem probable that the true importance of the lariat has nothing to do with either practical or decorative uses.

It is generally well known that, in the old days, as is still the case today, chuckwagons and campfires in the Occident were often ringed with cowboys engaged in scintillating conversation about recent poetry in the *New Yorker* or the *Weekly Gatherer*, news of a ballet or opera opening, or of some breakthrough in physics. What is less well known is that, at times, apparently by unspoken common consent, the cowboys moved a little apart from each other and spent half an hour, or perhaps many hours, in quiet, private thought.

Our strongest evidence of this practice comes from a fragment of a letter written by a cowboy, believed to be Carrasco van Deventer, who was employed on the Shumacher Ranch from about 1867 to at least 1883. The intended recipient of the letter is unknown.

Van Deventer writes,

> We just called it *moon-mulling*, because we did it more or less on schedule with the moon's phases—quarter moon, half moon, and so on. Randall Sanchez always sat cross-legged facing a mesquite stump. Alfonso Vela most generally hung from a live-oak branch, like he was going to chin himself. Valentine Finch, our foreman, stood just like a crane I saw once in Cabora Creek, with his left

leg drawn up. It was always his left leg, and he never moved. More than once the wind came up and blew him over, but he never noticed. We'd just prop him back up, and he'd go right on thinking. He was a deep thinker.

We never said much about these times to each other, and we for sure never talked about them to outsiders, but they meant a lot to us. They kind of helped us see the quiddity and quintessence of things, I guess you might say.

Anyway, the first notion we got that other crews were doing the same thing was when Numero Herrenmeyer came over from the Merton Ranch to work for us. One evening a couple of days after he came to camp it was time for moon-mulling. We didn't say anything to Numero, but just went ahead and started mulling. Valentine had already drawn up his left leg, and you could see he was a million miles away.

Numero watched us for a little bit, and then he spoke up.

"Be durn," he said. "You have deefenings here too."

"Do what?" I said.

"Have deefenings. That's what you're doing, ain't it? Having a deefening."

"Ain't no such," I answered. "We're moon-mulling, and if you'd shut up, I'd like to get on with mine."

Numero scratched his head, and then he muttered, "Well, it sure looks like a deefening to me."

Van Deventer's letter ends at this point, but anthropologists who have studied the Occident exhaustively have concluded that *deefening* is a shortened form of *dephenomenalizing*, that is, the practice of shifting, through deep thought, from the phenomenal world of the senses—the bellowing cows, horse manure, biting dust, boiled coffee, and barren vistas of the cowboys' daily existence—to the purer, noumenal world of intellectual forms. It is believed that Oliver Merton himself, the owner of the Merton Ranch at the time Herrenmeyer worked there, first coined the term for what he saw happening among his crew, and which he perhaps also participated in.

By far the most advanced form of the practice, however, appears to have occurred on the Kalplish Ranch, where it was called *lassoing*. Close observers were not surprised to learn that Miguel Cervantes, the fore-man of the ranch and the man generally acknowledged to be the lead-ing philosopher of the Texas Occident, was almost certainly the central figure of the activity there.

Cervantes apparently practiced lassoing from the start, perhaps as early as 1855, by sitting on the ground about twenty yards away from the camp-fire. He wore his hat, boots, and spurs, of course. His legs were crossed and re-crossed, and his feet were tucked over his thighs in a way that Mando Dirksen, a cowboy with the Kalplish outfit, was once heard to say, "looked like a square knot, and that's what we called it—the square knot position. His legs looked like they was plumb broke in about eight places." Cervantes always began lassoing shortly after dusk. Thumbs hooked in his belt on either side of the buckle, he sat erectly, looking neither left or right, and commonly remained in that position for three to five hours, although occasionally he might not move for a full day or more.

The first indication to Dirksen and other members of the Kalplish crew that Cervantes' powers of concentration might have actual physi-cal manifestations came while Cervantes was lassoing on a hot summer night in 1859, when, unnoticed by anyone until it was too late, a large diamondback rattlesnake crawled close to the foreman and coiled up in front of him. It reared up its head facing him, its rattles whirring and its tongue flicking out of its mouth.

"Don't shoot it," said Hurley Perkins, the wrangler, as several of the cowboys drew their guns. "I don't think Miguel would want us to."

Cervantes had not moved, even to blink. The cowboys, in fact, were not certain whether he was even aware of the deadly reptile before him.

Within a minute or so, the snake's rattling slowed, and then stopped. The rattler reared its head even higher, higher than any of the cowboys had ever seen a snake raise itself. Its tongue stopped flicking. It held

its body stiffly, swaying slightly from side to side, and rose ever higher until it towered over the peaked crown of Miguel's hat.

Suddenly the snake fell over backward, away from Miguel. Its body, Mando Dirksen said later, "was stiff as a bois d'arc post." Cervantes did not move; he remained as he was, in fact, for several hours after that. The snake lay belly up, and the cowboys thought it was dead. After about thirty minutes, however, it revived and crawled feebly off into the darkness. "It was yipping real soft," Dirksen said, "like a little ol' puppy when it's real scared."

The rattlesnake incident was never repeated. A few years later, however, an angrily tossed lariat resulted in an even more spectacular demonstration of Cervantes' powers. The Kalplish chuckwagon cook, Juan Dirksen, who was Mando's older brother, found a lariat someone had carelessly left on the tailgate of the wagon. He swore and threw it out into the darkness. It landed a few feet in front of Cervantes, who had been lassoing for about an hour.

Within minutes the rope began to uncoil and rise into the air.

"It looked just like that snake," Mando Dirksen said later. "The honda, or the eye of the rope, was just like its head, and it went up the same way."

The rope did not wriggle, but undulated gently from side to side until it reached a height of about ten feet. There it remained for a quarter of an hour, and then it slowly returned to the ground, neatly recoiling itself.

A few weeks later, to satisfy himself that what he had seen had really happened, Hurley Perkins put his own horse's favorite lariat in front of Miguel after the foreman had begun lassoing. The rope was sixty feet long. It had been dyed in bright pastel bands and was hung with hundreds of small silver bells.

Hurley's rope rose also, but it did not stop at ten feet. It rose steadily, swaying slightly, the bells tinkling pleasantly, until the entire rope was vertically suspended, with the lower end about three feet off the ground. It remained there for a few minutes while the cowboys watched speechlessly, glancing at each other to be sure they were all witnessing the same event.

"Then we heard a little sigh, and it just sailed on up out of sight," Mando Dirksen reported later. "It was just like a big hand had reached down from Ordnance Butte and snatched it up. But we heard the bells for a long time after it went."

Hurley Perkins never saw his rope again. There was, for a few months, some tension between him and Cervantes over the lost rope, although Miguel, when he arose from his square-knot position later, had no memory of the incident. He gave Hurley a new polka-dot lariat for Christmas that year, however, and patched up their friendship.

Others in the Kalplish outfit tried their hand at lariat-losing, as they called it, in later years. The word gradually shortened, first to *laroosing*, and finally to *lassoing*.

Reportedly, many of the cowboys became nearly as good at lassoing as Cervantes. It is persistently rumored, in fact, that sometime during the early 1880's, possibly in March or early April of 1882, as many as eight cowboys sent their ropes undulating up into the sky in a single night, and that forty ropes were lost in a single three-week period. While this report has never been confirmed, the records at Hubschrauber's General Store in Lindisfarne do show that the Kalplish Ranch was billed for five dozen new lariats on May 1, 1882. Also, a brief article in the *Weekly Gatherer* for the same week reported that Tad Kalplish I had fired several cowboys from his ranch crew. When a *Gatherer* reporter asked him why, he replied, "For thinking too damned much, that's why."

Before he accepts at face value any part of this account of meditation in the Texas Occident, the reader is warned that much of the information about these practices has been sifted from the mounds of nonsense, rumor, and hearsay left by D.D. McDougal, a man who must be considered as anything but a reliable source.

D.D. McDougal, of course, was the illiterate Texas Occident cattle rustler, Dangerous Dirk McDougal, the same man who, in 1902, suggested that ranchers increase their profits, and his, by castrating their male calves so they would gain weight faster. For this disgusting and, to Occidentals, inconceivable idea, he was banished from the Occident for life plus fifty years by the Lindisfarne Court of Absolutely No Appeal. He moved to New York City, became a mugger, and eventually formed McDougal and Associates, the highly successful literary agency. Although he never learned to read or write, he dictated to his secretary, a young Wellesley graduate, his "True History of the Texas Occident," as he called it. This "history" consisted of short, formless, untitled, and ungrammatical pieces about life in the Occident, particularly about more arcane matters such as the alleged practice of lassoing on the Kalplish Ranch. McDougal sent his work to Monahans Macleoud, the editor of the Lindisfarne *Weekly Gatherer*, who not only refused to print any of the allegations but did not acknowledge receiving them. Macleoud explained many years later that he could not take the word of such an accomplished scoundrel, and that the missives were such a jumbled mess of scurrilous drivel that he could make no sense of them anyway. Fifty years after McDougal's death in 1932, fulfilling the wish he had often expressed, his secretary brought his ashes back to the Occident and had them scattered over the desert. This despite the objections of many environmentalists and of the Occident citizenry in general, for whom McDougal's name remains anathema to this day.

Two further bits of evidence, one from the Kalplish Ranch and one from outer space, may have some bearing on the authenticity of McDougal's and van Deventer's accounts of lassoing.

In 1968 Tad Kalplish III, desiring to modernize and streamline the operations of his ranch, brought a Mercator-Martin Scat helicopter to the ranch and offered a substantial raise in wages to all or any of his cowboys who would learn how to pilot it. To his surprise, not a single cowboy volunteered. Everyone of them, in fact, flatly refused even to ride in it.

"How come?" Kalplish asked the assembled crew in the bunkhouse. "This would make all our work easier. How come none of you want to learn to fly the damned thing?"

Jesus Perkins ambled over to the window and peered out at the helicopter. It sat before the ranchhouse next to Kalplish's Mercedes, painted, like the Mercedes, in gleaming silver and maroon, the Kalplish Ranch colors.

"Well, Tad, I'll tell you," Jesus said, stroking his goatee. "It's on account of them big old whirly blades. We figure there's a lot of ropes hanging up in the sky somewhere over this ranch. Sooner or later, they're bound to get wrapped up something awful in them blades."

The other cowboys in the bunkhouse nodded solemnly, and no more was said. The next day Kalplish called the dealer in Lindisfarne and told him to come get his helicopter.

The other evidence involves the often whispered about but never publicly discussed *Rope Syndrome*, which was discovered—indeed, the only official communication ever sent from space about it was from him—by Evgeni Onegin, the Russian cosmonaut who was in the Soviet Union's orbital endurance program in 1975. One night in November of that year, Onegin radioed the Soviet Command Central with some startling information.

"You will think that I am losing my mind," Onegin said, "but I must tell you what I have just seen. Off to my right I saw several hundred ropes. They appeared to be lariats, such as the American cowboys use. They were extended to full length, and were brightly colored, some in stripes, others banded. They had bells and other knickknacks attached to them. They were nearly motionless, but seemed to undulate slightly. They were in a radically elliptical orbit—"

"*Nyet*, Evgeni, we do not think you are losing your mind," Command Central broke in. "We think you have lost it. We are bringing you down immediately."

After a long vacation, Onegin, his space career finished, was sent to teach junior high science in Nordvik. Since his radio transmission from space, no cosmonaut from any country has publicly acknowledged having any experience with the Rope Syndrome. Many, however, are said to have discussed it in whispers among themselves, and it remains one of the mysteries of outer space exploration.

Except, of course, to the practitioners of lassoing in the Texas Occident.

SIX-GUN V
Glorification of
Gunfighters Too Tough to Die

Although some of the expectant tension had lessened three decades after the Sanchez-Hamaker Gunfight began—"very few ladies walk around with their fingers in their ears any more," the *Weekly Gatherer* noted—the citizens were nevertheless proud of the two brave men who had been locked in mortal combat for over thirty years in the street between the Sotol Saloon and Hubschrauber's General Store.

The Chamber of Commerce built a fence around Randall Sanchez and Cesar Hamaker in the summer of 1905 and named the little area Gunfight Park. Five years later, in a burst of civic pride, the Chamber had pedestals sculpted for the two men, "fitting foundations," the *Weekly Gatherer* editorialized, "for our living statues, who may burst into explosive activity at any moment."

"You're going to mess up my aim," Cesar protested when he was lifted onto his base, "I had my feet dug in just right." But both men appeared a little vain about their new prestige, and they occasionally peeked down at their gleaming marble pedestals with more than casual pride.

Augustus Kalplish, having found in Idaho in 1894 the eldest Clinn-jin heir, Oren, who did not have the keys, had run into increasingly baffling obstacles in the years after that. He wrote to Valentine Finch in 1905, after admitting that he had not found a single Clinnjin sibling other than Oren, "It is as though some omniscient and omnipotent force is observing me and my movements. Whatever I do to find the keys that would enable Cesar Hamaker to shoot Randall Sanchez is frustrated.

If I am approaching a town where, say, one of the daughters had been living for fifteen years, huge trees fall across the road in front of me; bridges collapse minutes before I reach them; and when at last I come to the town, the daughter and her entire family have packed up and left without a trace. Records disappear. Photographs are altered. Names are changed. I am at my wits' end."

Kalplish never found another of Cal Clinnjin's children.

In 1921, two decades after the first winter of Hamaker Howls, rumors began to circulate in Lindisfarne that were eventually confirmed by Monahans Macleoud I, the son of the famed bootmaker Angus Macleoud and the editor of the *Weekly Gatherer*. The rumors were started by revelers returning to Lindisfarne late at night from outings to a spot fifteen miles north of town, where they pretended to see a fictitious phenomenon known as the Martha Lights. Cesar Hamaker howled, the rumors went, because he was, indeed, lonely. He was lonely because, for several hours four nights out of every week, the other pedestal in Gunfight Park was empty.

Hidden behind a Sotol Saloon garbage can, Macleoud waited and shivered night after night until finally he saw, emerging from a secret door at a corner of Hubschrauber's General Store, which by now was quite shabby and desolate-looking, a tall, broad-shouldered figure in a long dress. For a moment Macleoud was puzzled, for despite the freezing temperature, he thought he saw large butterflies flitting around the woman. Then he realized they were bows. The woman looked carefully in every direction; then she darted into the park and grabbed Randall Sanchez, who was virtually weightless from his long vigil.

"Now Betsy, you hadn't ought—" Monahans I heard Randall protest.

"You hush." The woman tucked Randall under her arm, his legs still spread in their alert crouch, his hands still poised over his box holsters. Then she ran back to the secret door and disappeared.

Half a minute later, Cesar Hamaker's howl rent the still night air.

Sensitive to the delicate needs of many people and to the higher good of the Texas Occident, Macleoud never printed the story of what he saw that night. He did, however, confront Betsy Hubschrauber with what he had seen. At first she denied all; but then, knowing Monahans I to be a concerned and discreet friend, and unable to bear the weight of the many secrets she had carried for so many years, she broke down. Over the next several months, Monahans I learned, and recorded in his personal journal, the astounding stories behind the story of the Sanchez-Hamaker Gunfight.

In her love for Randall Sanchez, Betsy had striven desperately to help Leticia Harnsgartner's mother find her son, and therefore the keys that would spell the death of Cesar Hamaker. So she had poured in, always anonymously, untold sums of money in the search for Amos Harnsgartner, the banker who had disappeared with Randall's keys.

In 1886, however, when it became apparent that Randall Sanchez's keys might not be found for many more years, Betsy thought that, with the seemingly boundless income from her store, she could also influence the search for the other set of keys, Cesar Hamaker's keys. That is, she might see to it that they were never found, or at any rate never returned to Lindisfarne, where they would be used to destroy her beloved Randall.

So she hired her own agents, and she learned of Cal Clinnjin's death a full year before Augustus Kalplish did. She was able to hide the whereabouts of all the Clinnjin heirs except the eldest, Oren. In time her agents narrowed the search for the keys to the two youngest daughters, Amanda, who was a civil engineer in Cleveland, and Calvina, a wildcatter in the oil fields of the Spindletop area of East Texas. In 1913, enthralled by the fairytale landscape of the area, Calvina moved to Odessa, Texas, which was barely 200 miles from Lindisfarne. There Betsy's agents found her, and Cesar Hamaker's keys, in 1916. Within three days, aided by a huge bribe, the agents persuaded Calvina to weld Cesar's keys to an early version of a rotary drill bit. With Betsy herself present to watch, the bit was lowered to 4,180 feet and ground against a layer of solid granite until the very bit itself was no more.

"I returned home delirious with happiness," Betsy told Monahans Macleoud I, "for my beloved Randall was safe. At first I meant to tell him right away that he was safe, he could sit down, lie down, take a bath like an ordinary man. But something told me not to, and when my early euphoria had drained away I realized what I had done. I understood that, if the story ever got out that the life of Randall Sanchez, Randall Sanchez of the most famous gunfight ever fought, had been saved by a scheming, sneaking woman, that he would never forgive me, or himself."

So she said nothing, and continued to carry him upstairs to her warm bed while Cesar Hamaker howled outside. In 1919, a few months after the end of World War I, when Betsy's vast bank account was almost empty, one of Leticia Harnsgartner's mother's agents, who were all really double agents now, for they reported both to Leticia's mother, and unknown to her, to Betsy also, found Amos Harnsgartner working as an elephant tender in the foothills of the Indian Himalayas. He had Randall Sanchez's toxbox keys dangling from a gold chain around his neck, the last evidence of his ill-gotten gains. The agent quickly negotiated for the keys, and the chain too, and, after first notifying Betsy, boarded a ship for the journey home.

By now Betsy, having long anticipated the finding of Randall's keys, had realized that while she could not right the wrong she had perpetrated on Cesar Hamaker, and therefore on Randall Sanchez too, she could equalize the wrongs. She sent a wire to her agent, and as his ship, taking the eastern route home, crossed the Marinas Trench near Guam, he dropped the chain and the keys into water more than six miles deep.

Monahans Macleoud I had a great story, but his loyalty to the traditions and dignity of the Texas Occident would not let him print it, at least as long as the two brave and determined men stood on their marble pedestals between Hubschrauber's General Store and the Sotol Saloon awaiting the keys to unlock the boxes which would enable them to send hot-leaded death at each other—the keys that would never come. So they have stood there, crouched, alert, and ready, as the decades have gone by.

And they're still there today.

GLOSSARY

BACTRIAN HEREFORD—A breed of desert cattle which uses the two humps on its back to condense water from the desert air and to cool the body. It prefers cactus and mesquite thorns to all other food.

BARBSHOPS—Studios where artisans design the barbs for barbed wire fences.

BIBLE BELT—A belt with a compartment built into the omphalos which is large enough to contain a Bible.

BOX-HOLSTER—A scabbard for a toxbox.

BRANDPAINTING—The practice of painting intricate, highly artistic designs on the flanks of cows.

BUCKING SCHOOL—(TOBS, or Texas Occident Bucking School) An institute located near Lindisfarne, Texas. It was founded in 1869 for the purpose of teaching horses to buck.

BULLET BUCKLE—A very small, round omphalos, usually no more than 3/4" in diameter.

BULLET-RIDDLED—A popular hat style in the Texas Occident.

CACTUS WHEEL—A sharp-pointed rowel installed on a spur for masochistic purposes.

CALF INSPECTION—A periodic inspection once proposed as a means of discovering those cowboys believed to be spurgellants. It was never carried out.

CHIHUAHUAN SHORTHORN—A breed of desert cattle characterized by extremely short hair and short, horn-like protuberances over much of its body. Also called the Toad Cow. It feeds primarily at night, remaining in the shade under brush or large rocks during the hot desert days.

CONVEYER BELT—A belt with a profound message engraved on its omphalos.

CUTTING HORSE—A witty, sharp-tongued horse with a malicious, "cutting" sense of humor.

DEEFENING—See Lassoing.

DESERT HEREFORD—A very tall, very thin breed of desert cattle. To conserve energy and water during the hottest hours of the day, it exposes only the thinnest part of its body to the sun, thus casting a shadow no wider than a strand of baling wire. It feeds on yucca spears.

EARMUFFS—Wide-flapped leather garments, sometimes with the hair left on and/or highly decorated, which cowboys in the Texas Occident wear over their jeans, purportedly to protect their legs.

FLAGHORSE—The foremost horse, usually chosen for its intellect, high moral character, and seniority, in a retinue of horses being trailed. Flaghorses, once they are so designated, retain their position for life and are always carried.

FLAMBOYANT—A popular hat style.

FRUIT BOOT—The standard footwear of the Texas Occident. A boot with a tall, highly decorated top, a vamp which tapers to a point and crushes the toes, and a high Cuban heel which makes walking difficult if not dangerous.

GRAIN BELT—See Bible Belt.

HAMAKER HOWL—An utterance much resembling the howl of the timber wolf, but more prolonged and of a ghastlier pitch. In the Texas Occident, it is understood to be an expression of loneliness and/or general dissatisfaction with one's present circumstances.

HAT-WINDMILL—A spur.

HEROIC—A popular hat style.

HEX DAGGER—See Cactus Wheel.

HORNHAT DECADE—The decade, believed to have been from about 1910 to 1920, when many cowboys in the Texas Occident favored a Viking-like head covering which had horns from longhorn cattle attached to it.

HORSE-BEARER—An individual, usually a man chosen for his strength and stamina, who helps to carry a horse.

HORSE-SLINGING—A method of horse-bearing in which the horse is carried, usually upside-down, in a large leather or canvas sling.

HORSE-TRAILING—The practice, sometimes ceremonial and sometimes to please the animals, of carrying horses, either by hand or in trailers which are specially made for the purpose.

HOWDY—A precarious chair built on stilt-like legs and placed above the saddle on a horse.

KNOBITY—An advanced means of communication practiced by drivers on the roads of the Texas Occident.

LASSOING—General term for a form of deep meditation practiced by cowboys in the Texas Occident.

LYNCHING OF THE INSUFFERABLE IDEA—The only lynching which ever occurred in the Texas Occident. The idea could not be hanged, but its utterer could.

MACLEOUD'S HOLSTER GUM—A thick, stubborn glue used in holsters to prevent the gun owner from drawing his gun too quickly. It was never approved by the National Rifle Association.

MACLEOUD'S THUMB-ROT BALM—A substance developed by a pioneer Texas Occident bootmaker, Angus Macleoud, to combat a fungus which develops in thumbs when they are hooked in one's belt for more than twelve hours a day over a period of many years.

MARLBORO SESSIONS—Monthly training for cowboys who want to be in cigarette ads. Typical lessons include Square Jaw Profiling, Looking Inevitable While Sitting on a Corral Fence, and Introductory Leg Hooked over the Saddlehorn Posing.

MARTHA LIGHTS—For over a century in the Texas Occident it has been a form of social intercourse to drive outside of town in the middle of the night, park by the side of the road, scatter the antelope, and pretend to see the non-existent "Martha Lights" far off to the southwest. Thus the expression, "Show 'em the lights," meaning to simultaneously delude oneself and others.

MAYOR MIRANDA MITTEN—A heavy, stiff mitten which, for a short period in the nineteenth century, cowboys wore on their gunhand to protect their friends and enemies from too-hasty trigger-pulling.

MOON-MULLING—See Lassoing.

OMPHALOS—The large, oval-shaped metal disc used to fasten together the two ends of a cowboy's belt.

PICKUP—A vehicle which is valued in the Texas Occident for its impracticality, lack of economy, noise pollution, and ugliness. It is used to store empty beer cans.

PMS-DDDD, BHBCR, etc.—Various models of pickups which have been manufacturer-customized to the tastes of Texas Occident drivers. The PMS-DDDD, for example, is a GMC which has been Permanently Mud-Stained and pre-Dented in four places; the Dodge BHBCR has a mechanical Blue Heeler Balanced on the Cab Roof. The blue heeler is a species of Australian sheepdog which entered the country about the same time as Dutch Elm disease. It is equally obnoxious.

RANGE GRAFFITI—The vast body of literature, most of it poetry in rhyming trochaic heptameter couplets, which has been secretly and laboriously carved on boulders in the Texas Occident.

REPROACHFUL YEARS—A period lasting about a decade near the end of the nineteenth century when some young cowboys blamed themselves too severely for their youthful mistakes.

RODEO—A time of introspection and intellectual problem sharing and solving.

ROPE SYNDROME—A term used with reference to the sighting of lariats in outer space. Neither the Soviet nor American space program has ever acknowledged the existence of, or even rumors of, this phenomenon.

SADDLE—A leather contrivance, often decorated with original works of art, used to separate cowboys from their horses.

SENICULTURE—An overwhelming desire to plow up land that God clearly meant for cattle to graze on.

SHUMACHER SHAME AND TRUCULENCE DECADE—A period in the 1930's when the cowboys on the Shumacher Ranch were compelled to perform duties which they detested so much that they underwent temporary personality changes.

SPINY ANGUS—One of several breeds of desert cattle developed in the Texas Occident which are capable of subsisting comfortably for extended periods of time without water. It has a high, sharp, fin-like ridge running down its back. How long a Spiny Angus can go without water is not known, since no one has ever seen one drink. Some observers believe the Spiny Angus extracts moisture from desert rocks which it holds in its mouth.

SPUR—A device intended to help prevent cowboy homesickness. It was invented by the staff at Hubschrauber's General Store in Lindisfarne, Texas.

SPURGELLANTS—Contrite cowboys who punish themselves with their spurs.

SQUARE KNOT—A yoga-like position favored by some practitioners of lassoing in the Texas Occident.

STAR BLADE—See Cactus Wheel.

STRAND—Horses in the Texas Occident generally prefer this term for *lariat*.

SUN BELT—A belt with a large, blindingly bright omphalos.

TOSAPEO—Texas Occident Society Against Plugging Each Other.

TOXBOX—(Short for Texas Occident Boxes and Box Holsters) A box for holding a disassembled revolver.

TROJAN HORSE—A method of horse-bearing which requires ten strong men.

WINDMILL REMEMBRANCE YEARS—A period when the Texas Occident cowboy suffered overwhelming nostalgia for windmills after they became obsolete.

ABOUT THE AUTHOR

Roland Sodowsky is a native of Oklahoma who lived and taught for many years in West Texas and is now on the English faculty at Southwest Missouri State University. He is the author of *Things We Lose,* a volume of short stories, and he is the recipient of a National Endowment for the Arts creative-writing grant.

Michael Krone is a free-lance illustrator living in Austin, Texas.